Bohol: Around Tagbilaran in Pictures

Bohol: Around Tagbiliaran in Pictures

Rob Benton

Esotericom®

All photographs by Rob Benton

ISBN 978-0-9980682-7-5

He stood, and measured the earth:
He beheld, and drove asunder the nations;
and the everlasting mountains were scattered,
the perpetual hills did bow:
His ways are everlasting.

--Habakkuk 3:6

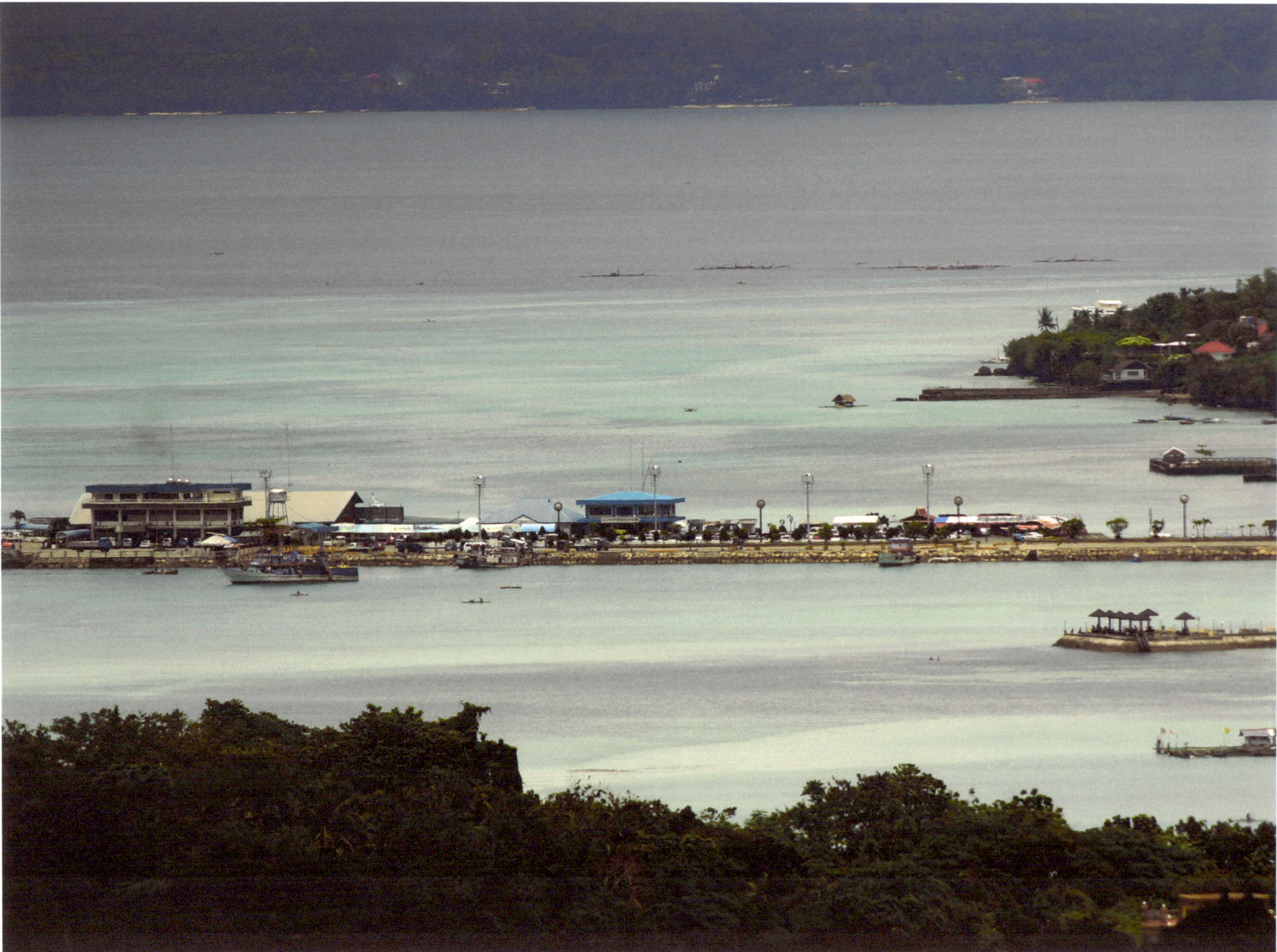

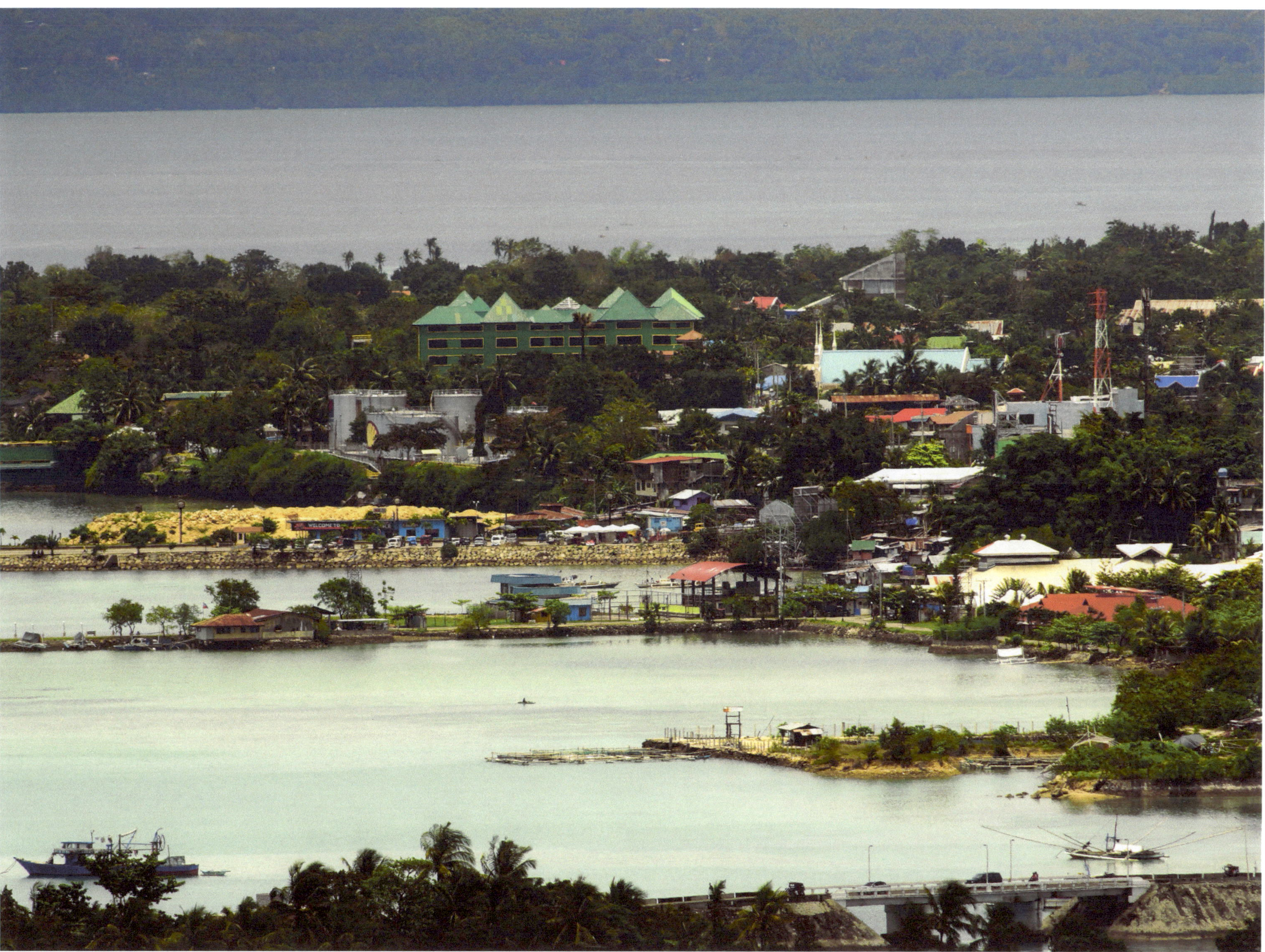
WELCOME TO

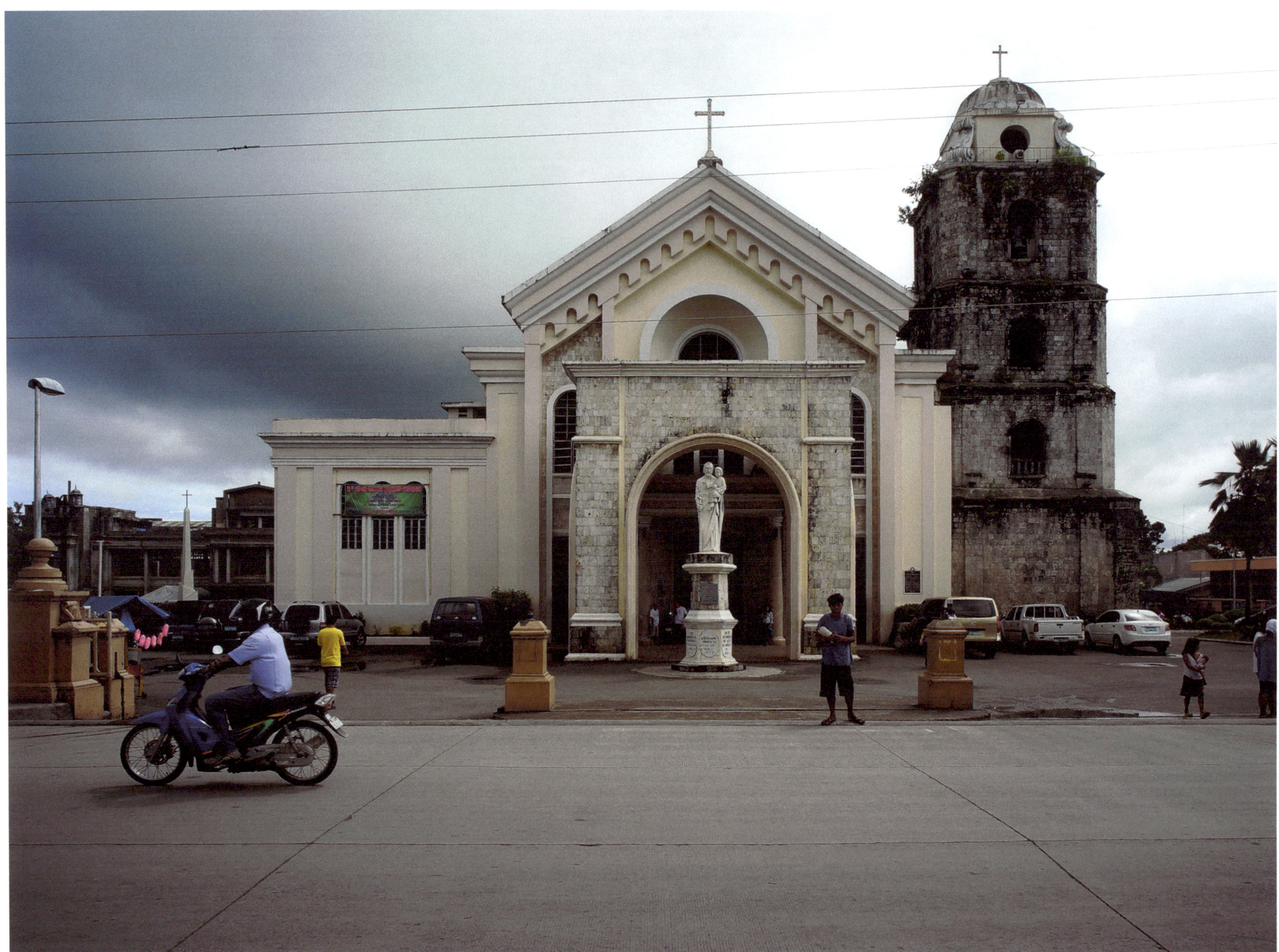

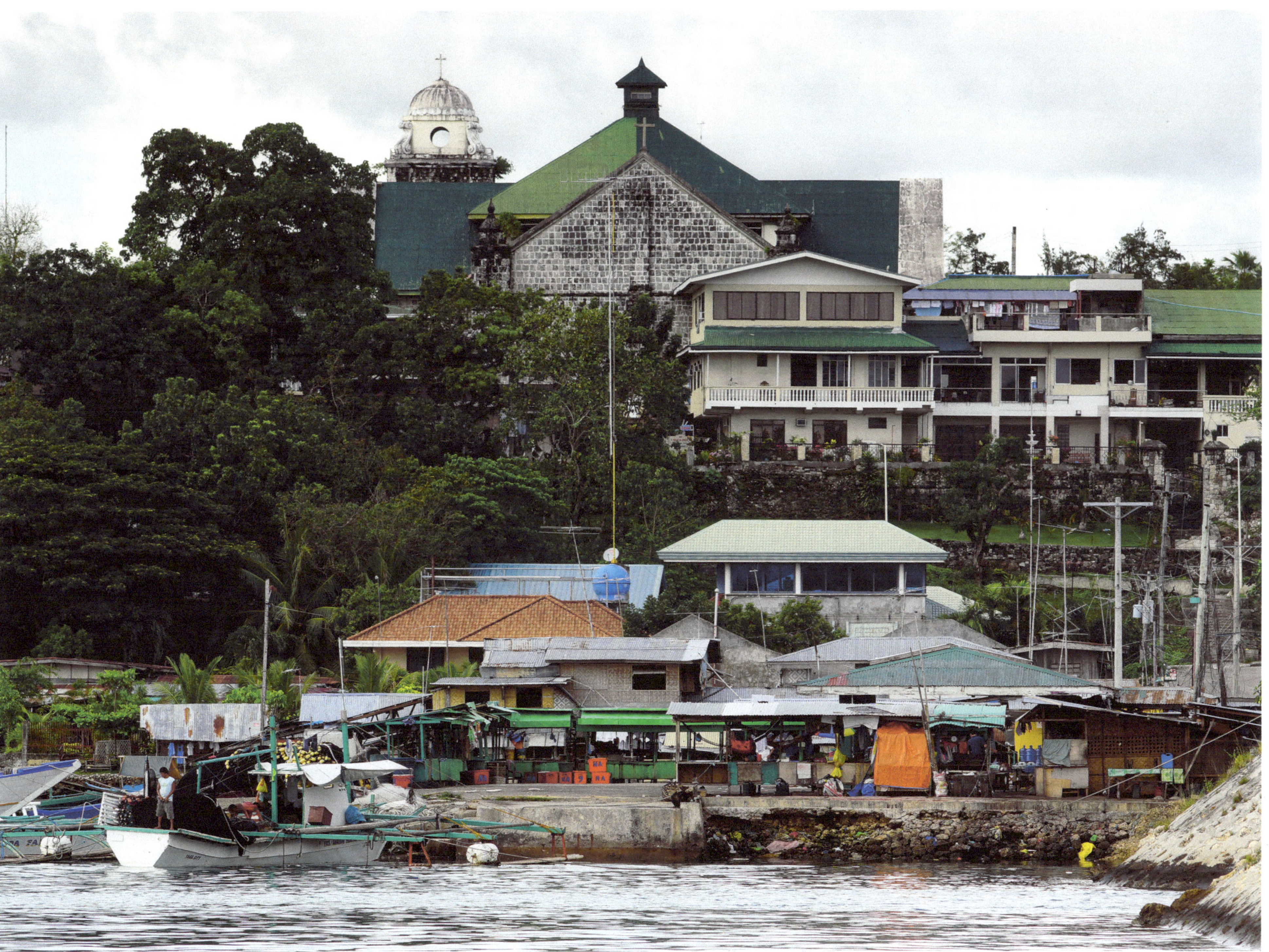

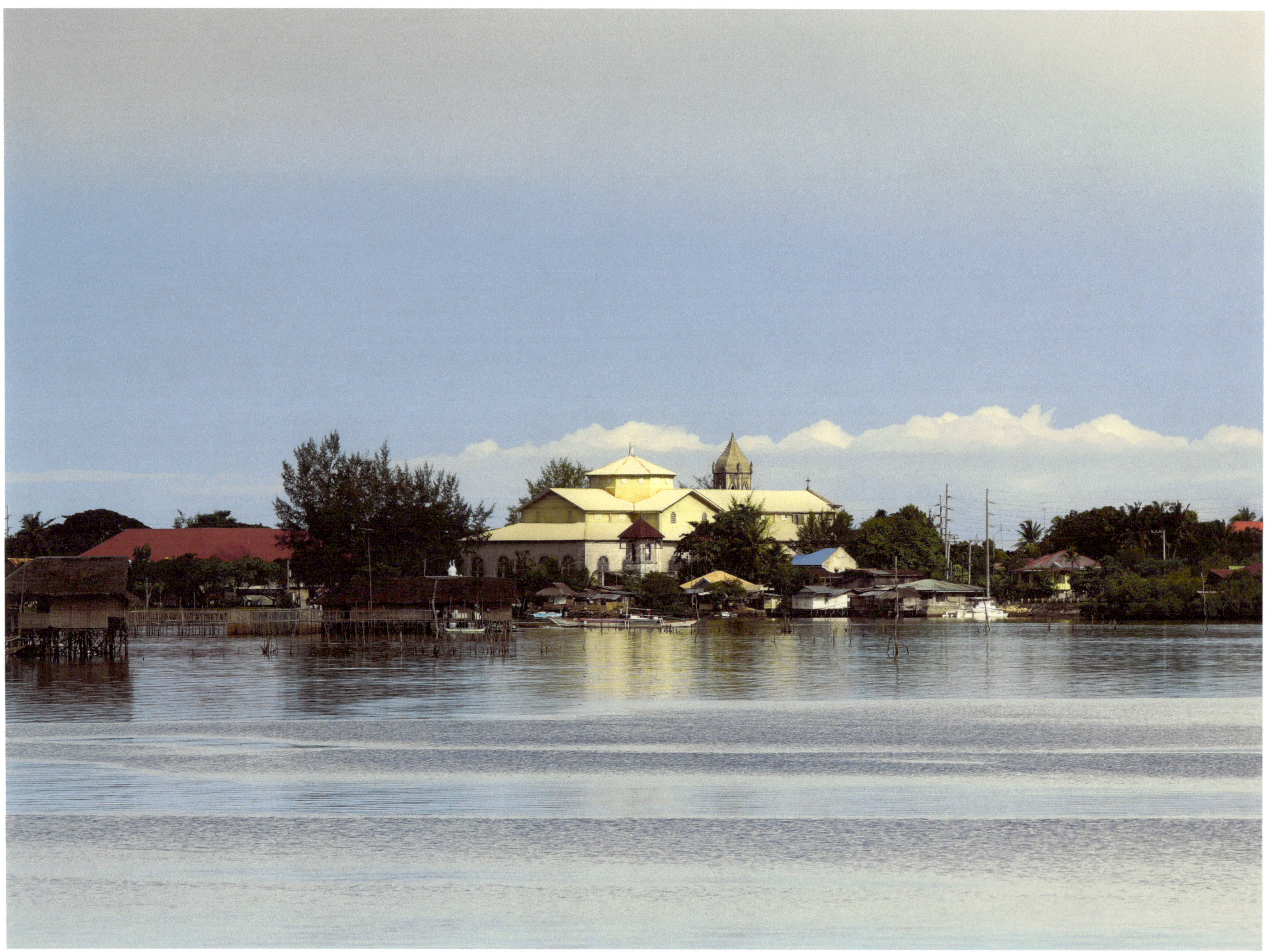

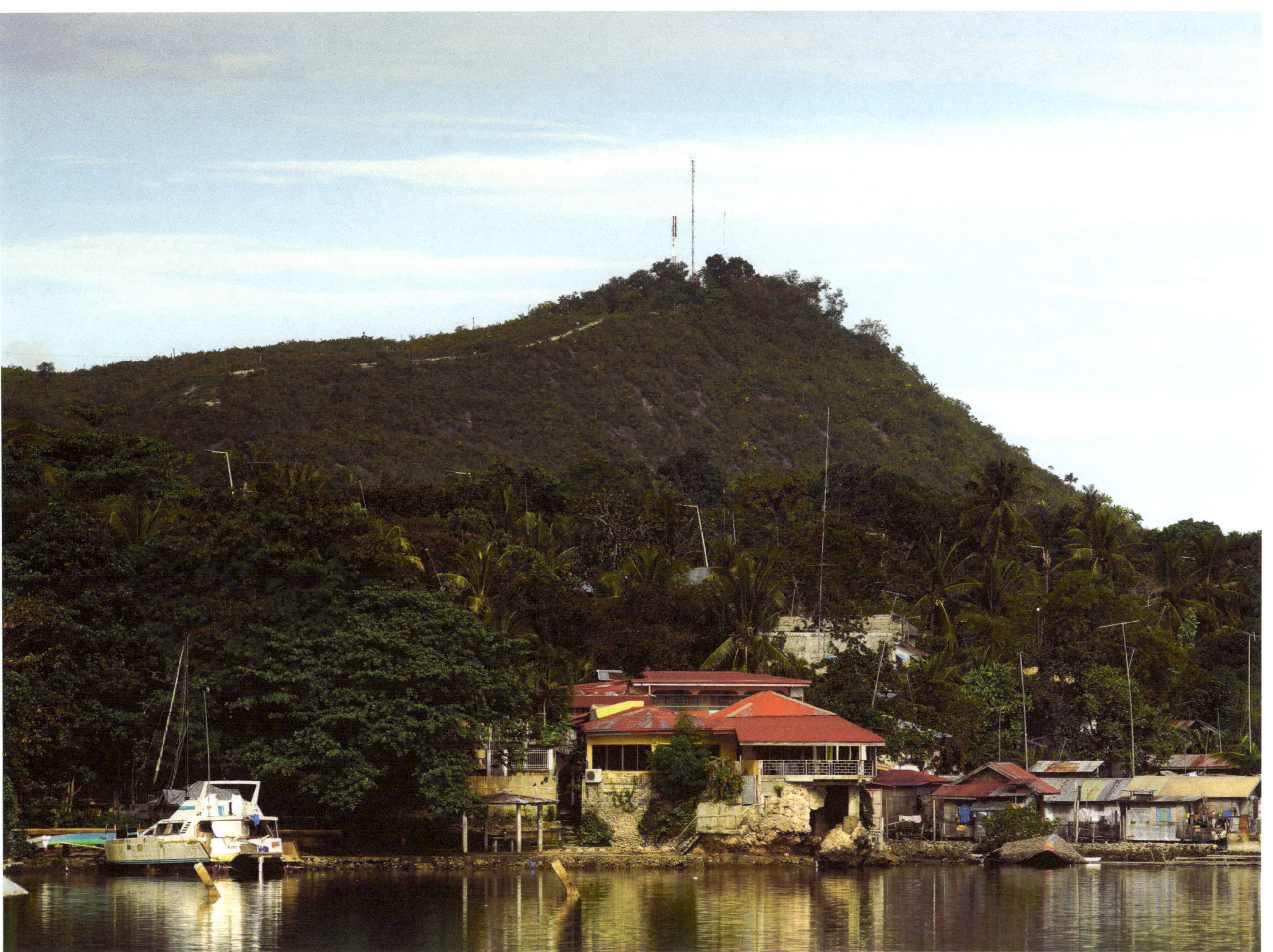

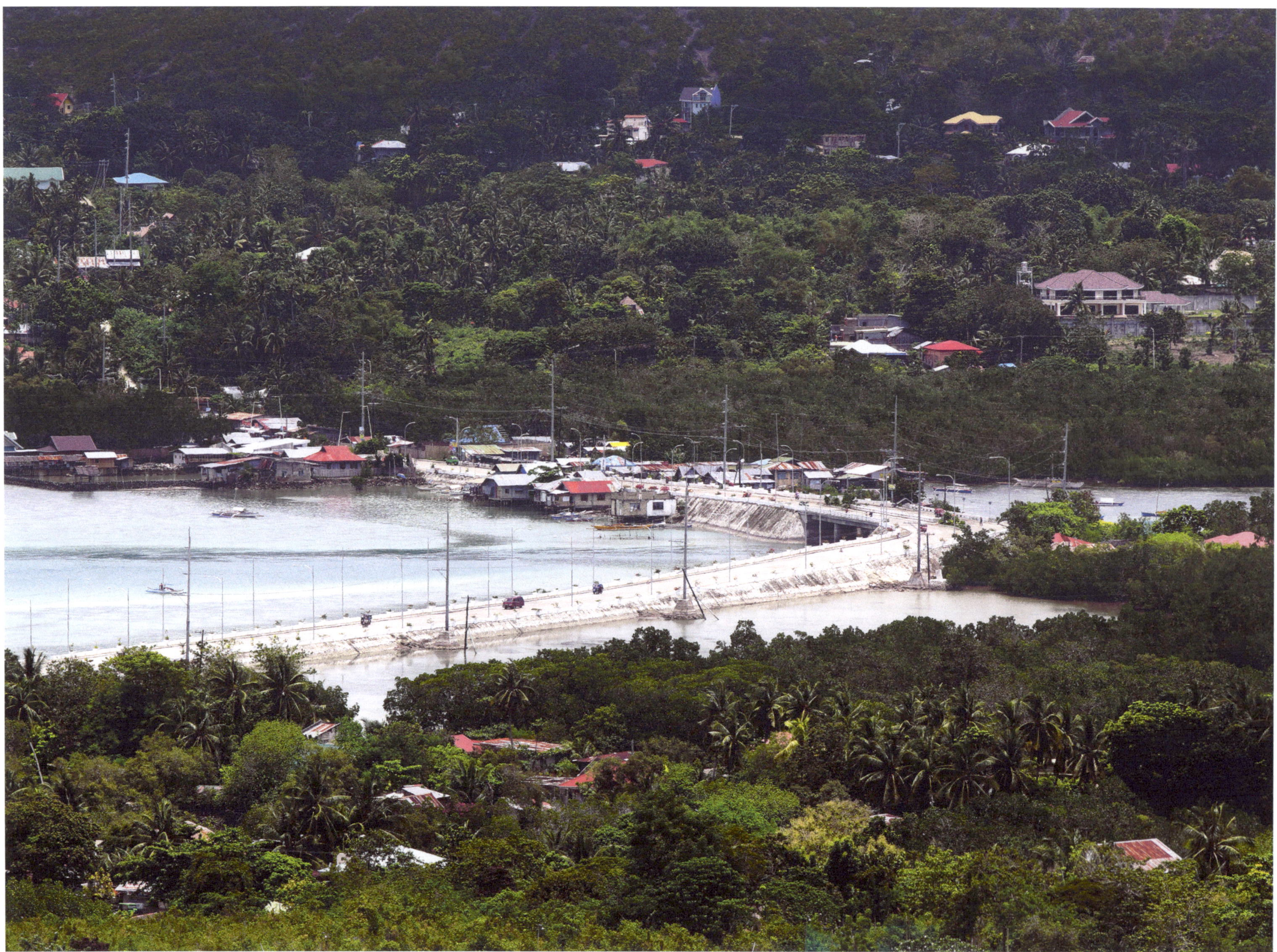

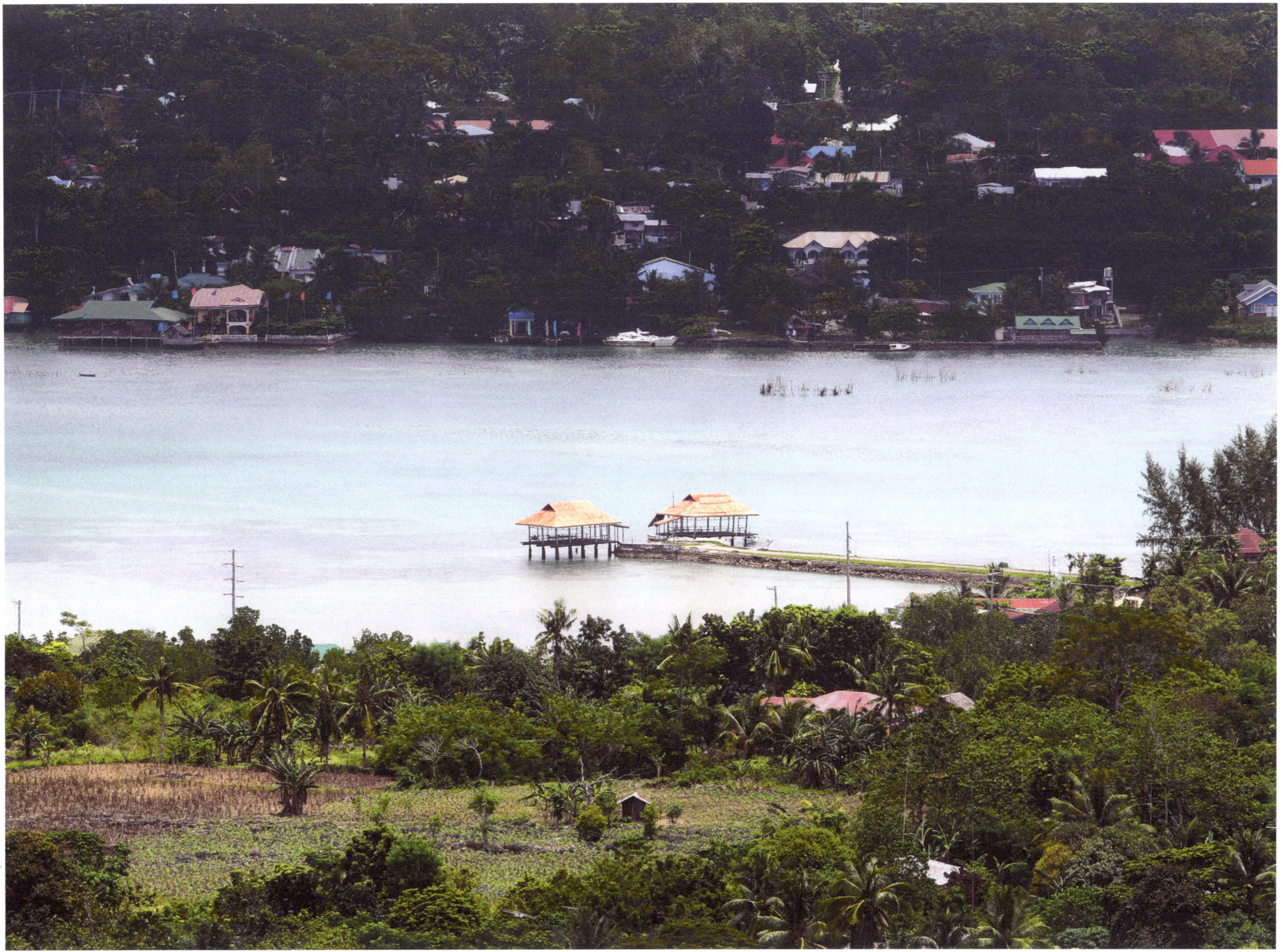

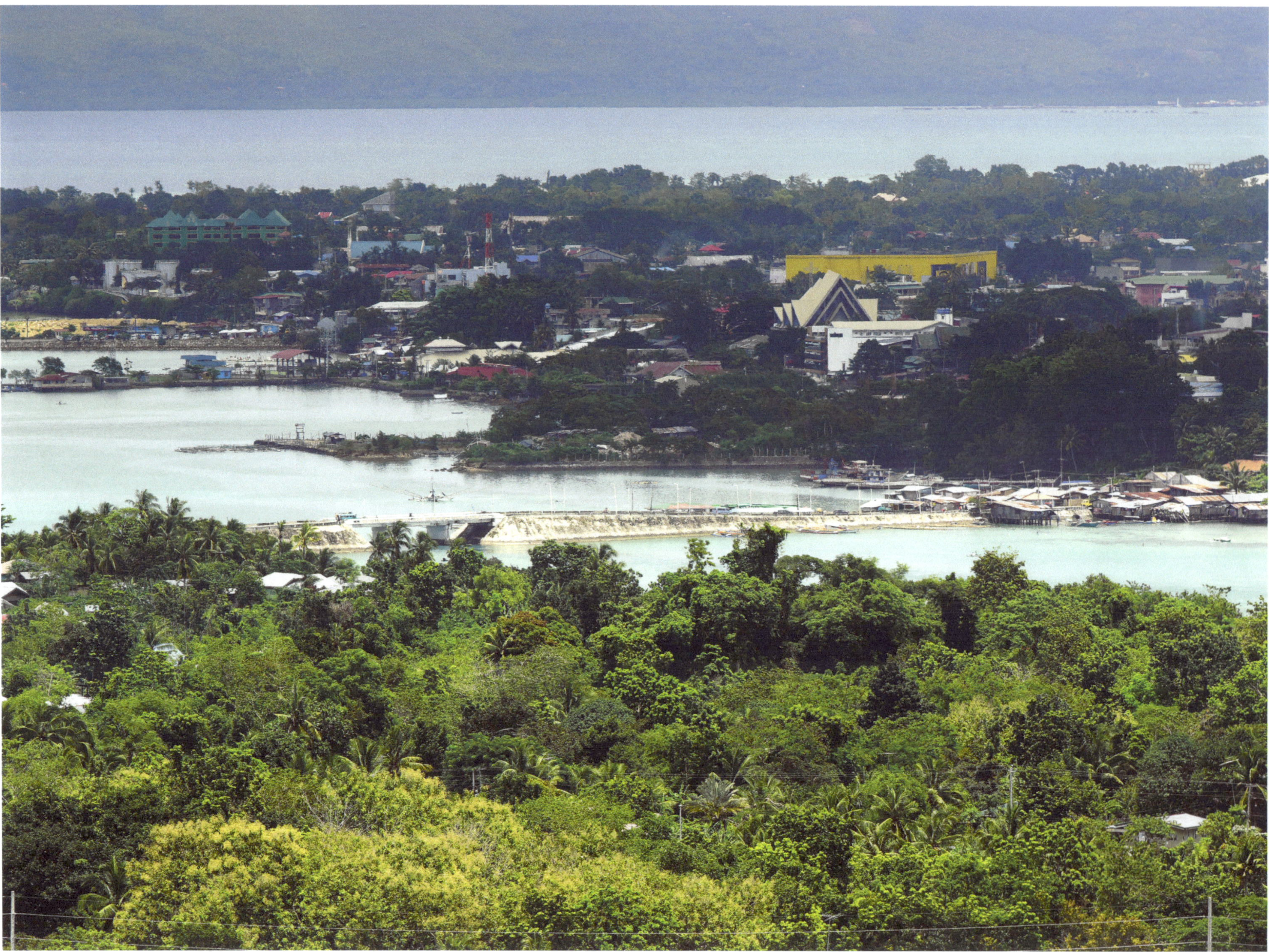

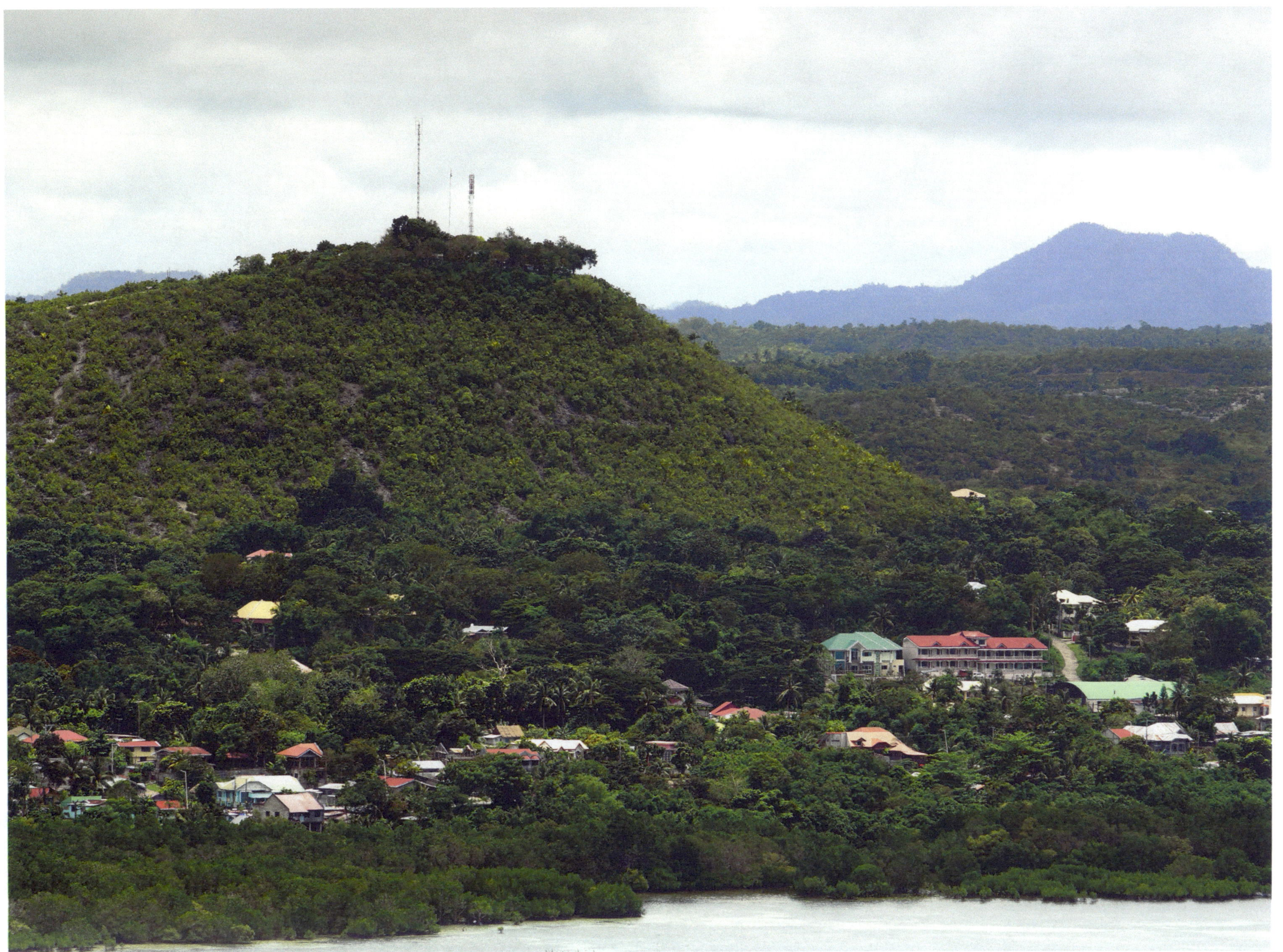

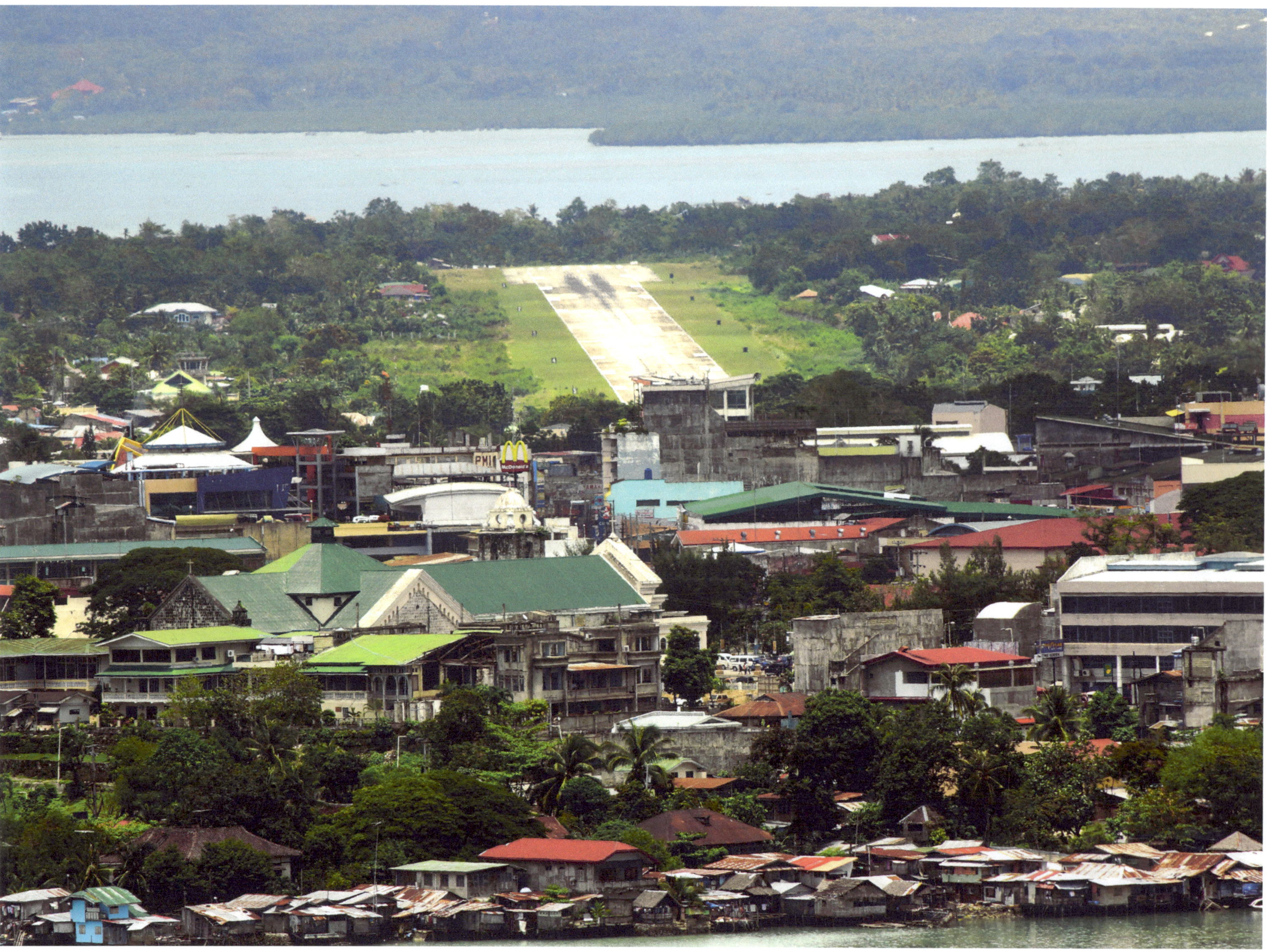
PMI
McDonald's

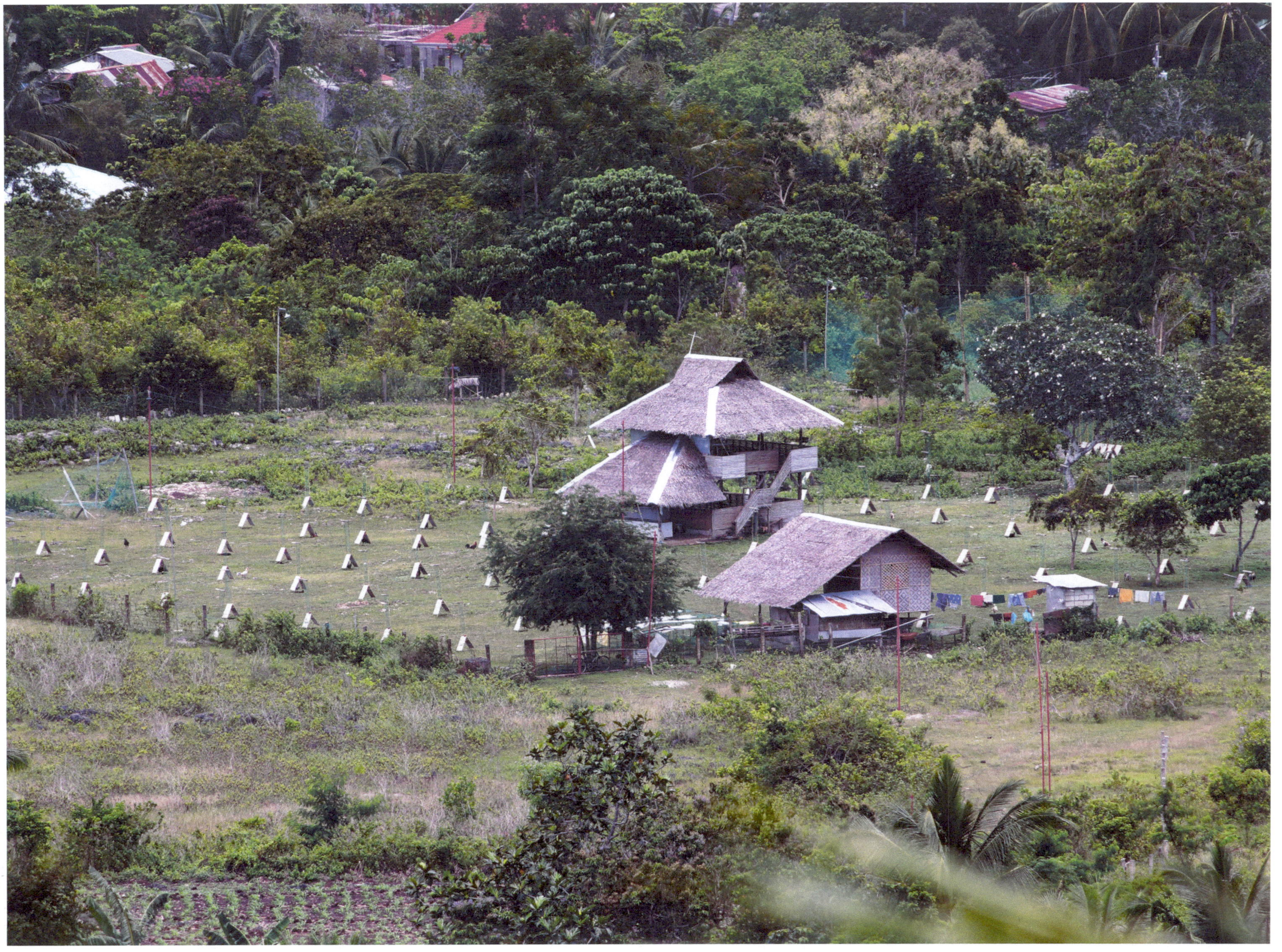

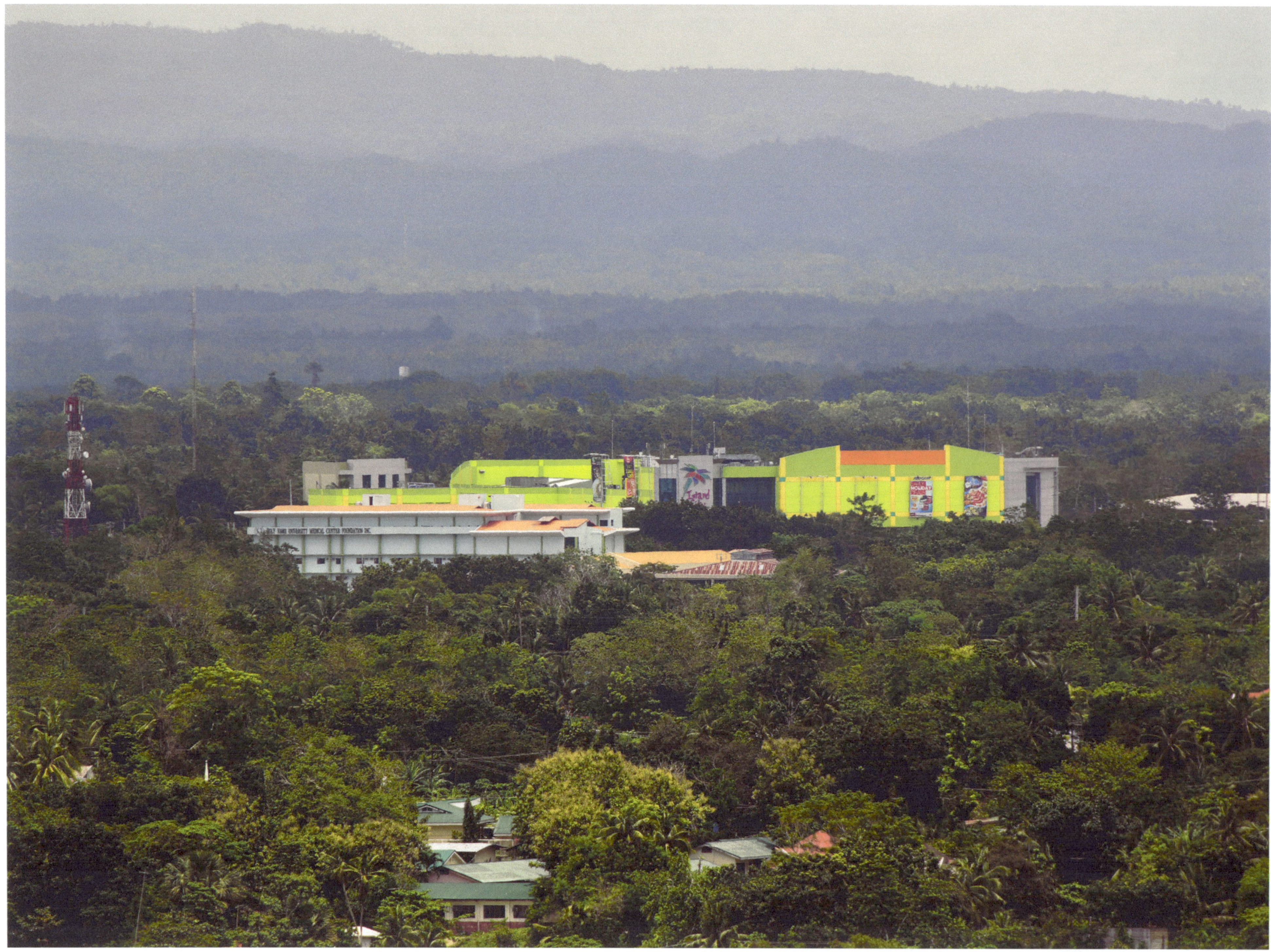
Island
HOLIDAY

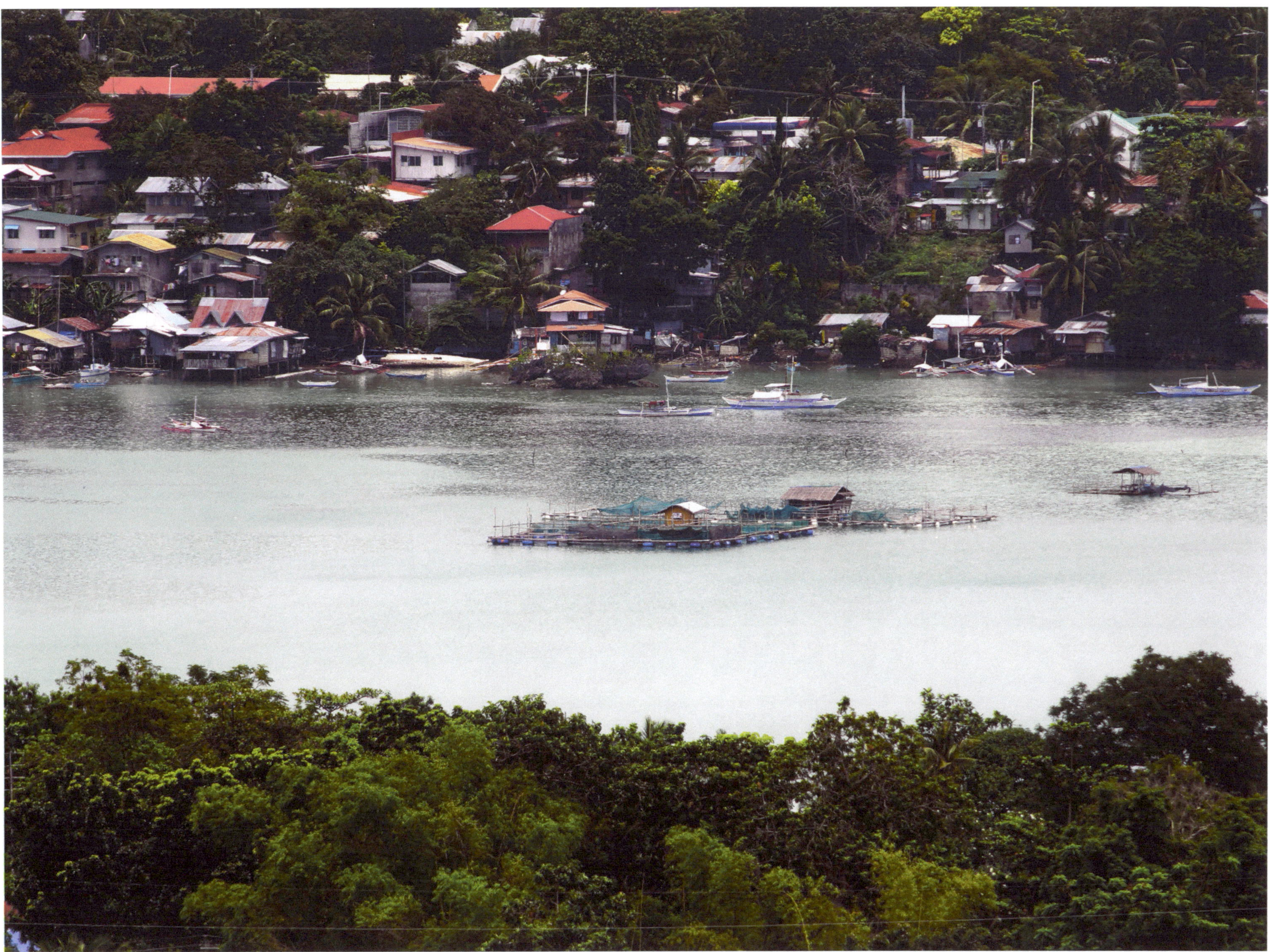

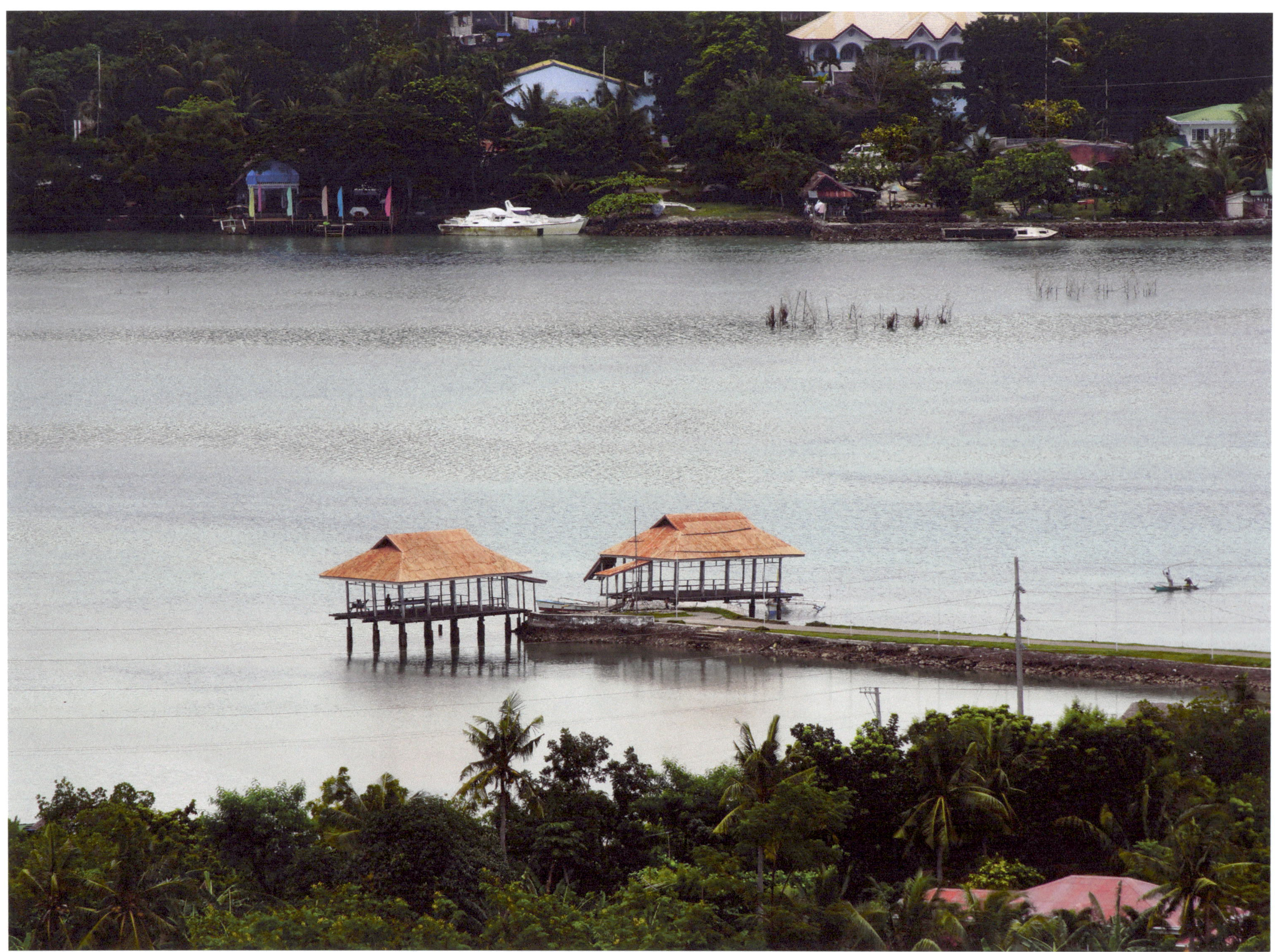

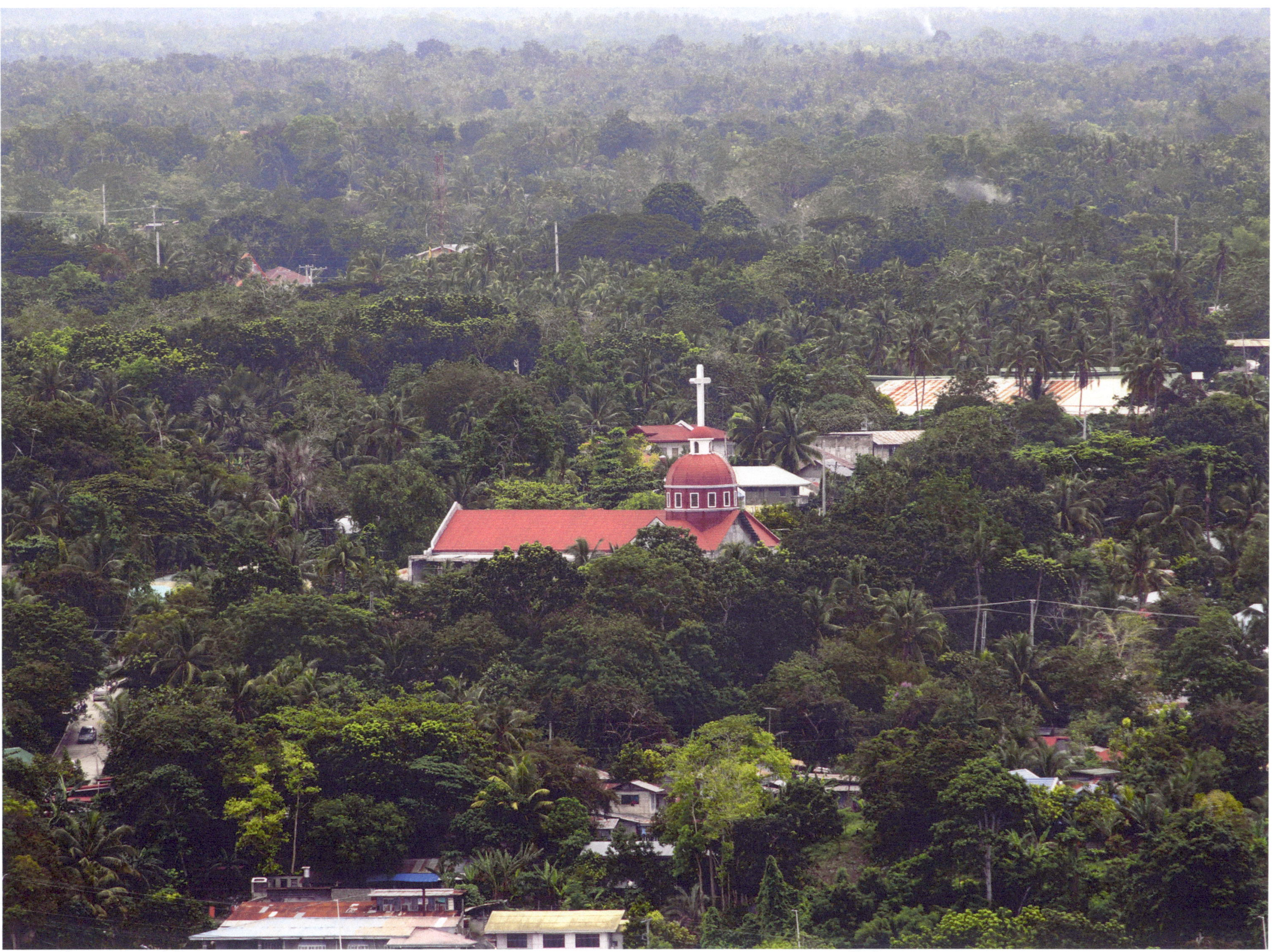

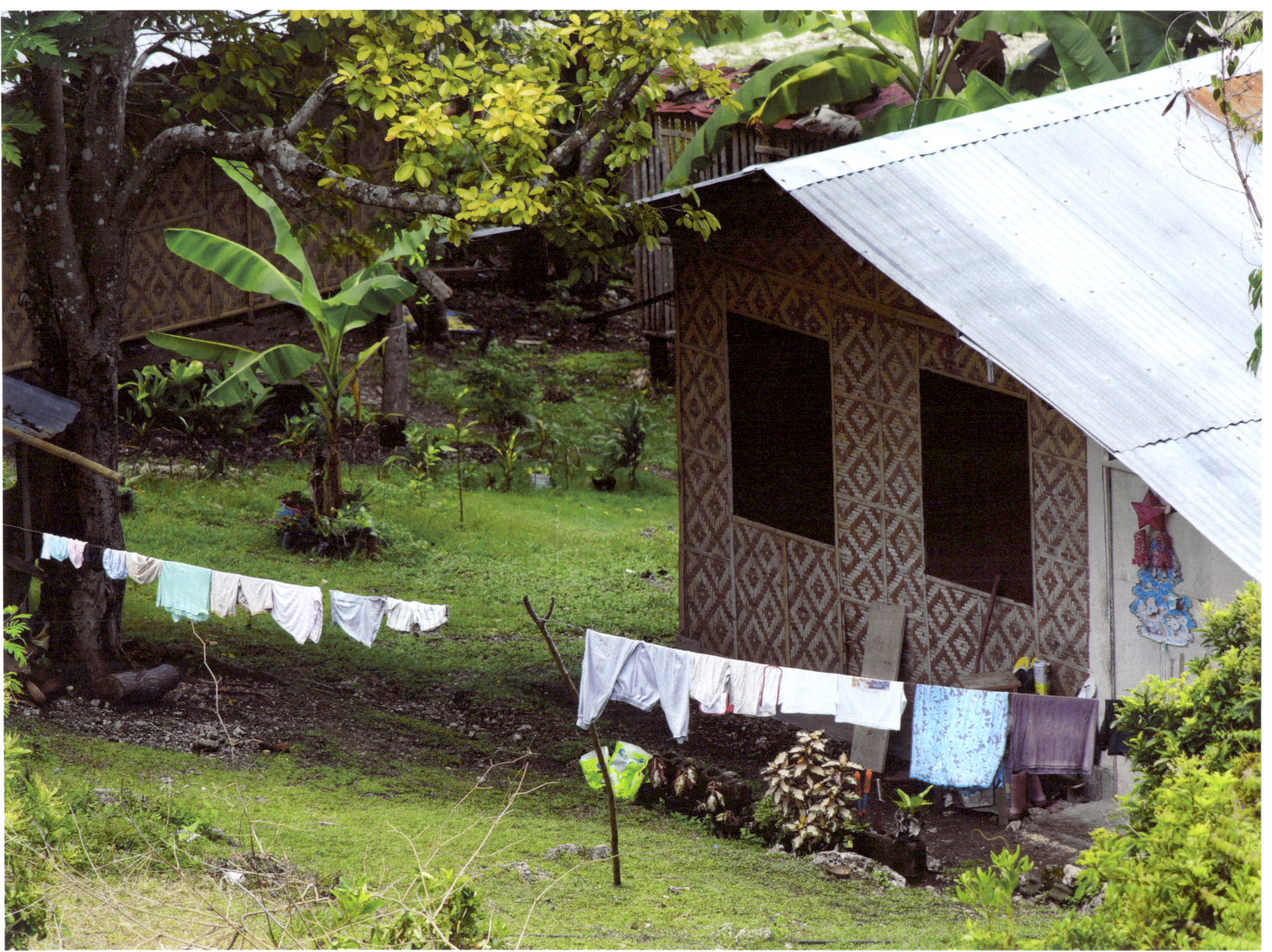

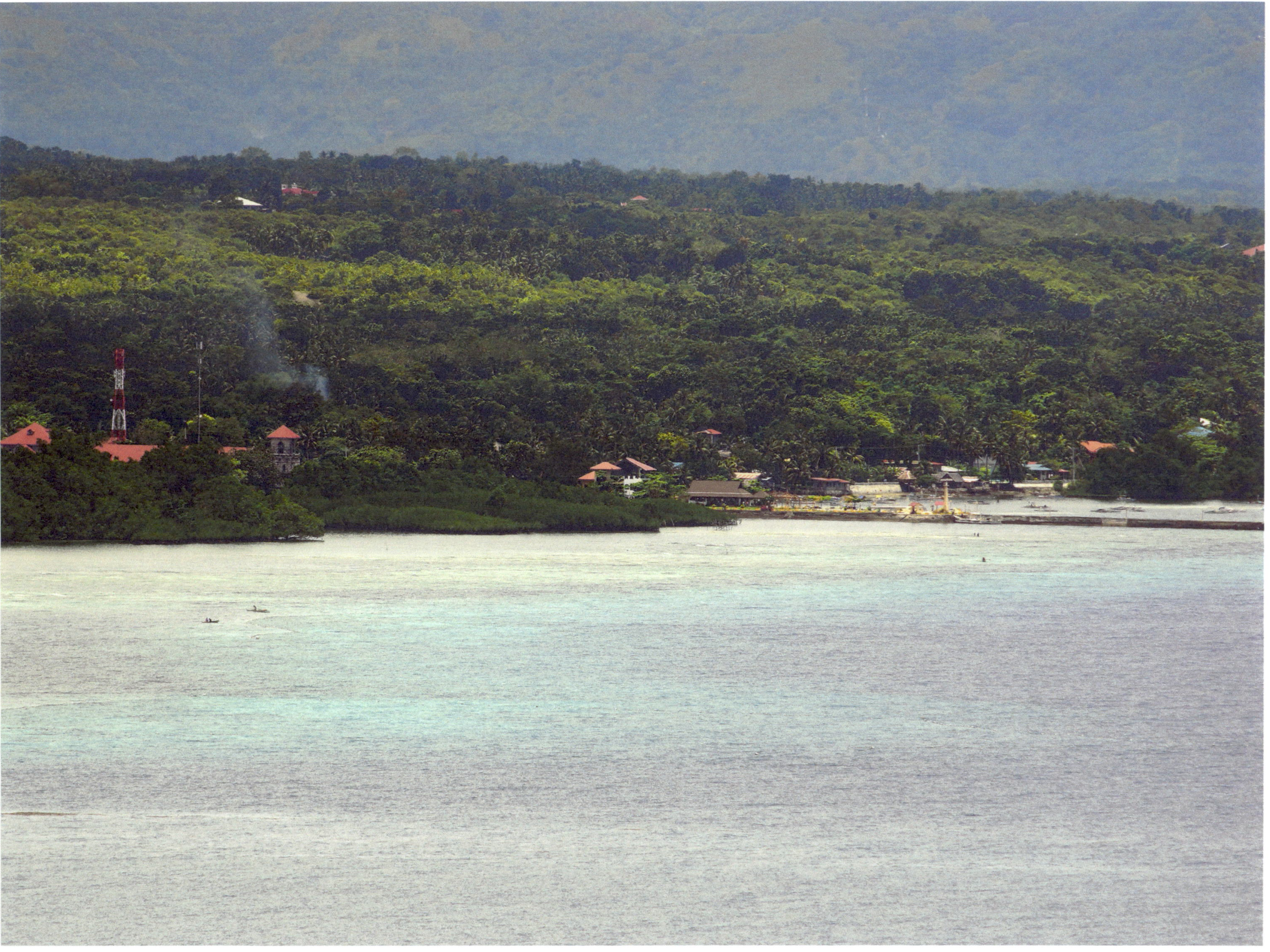

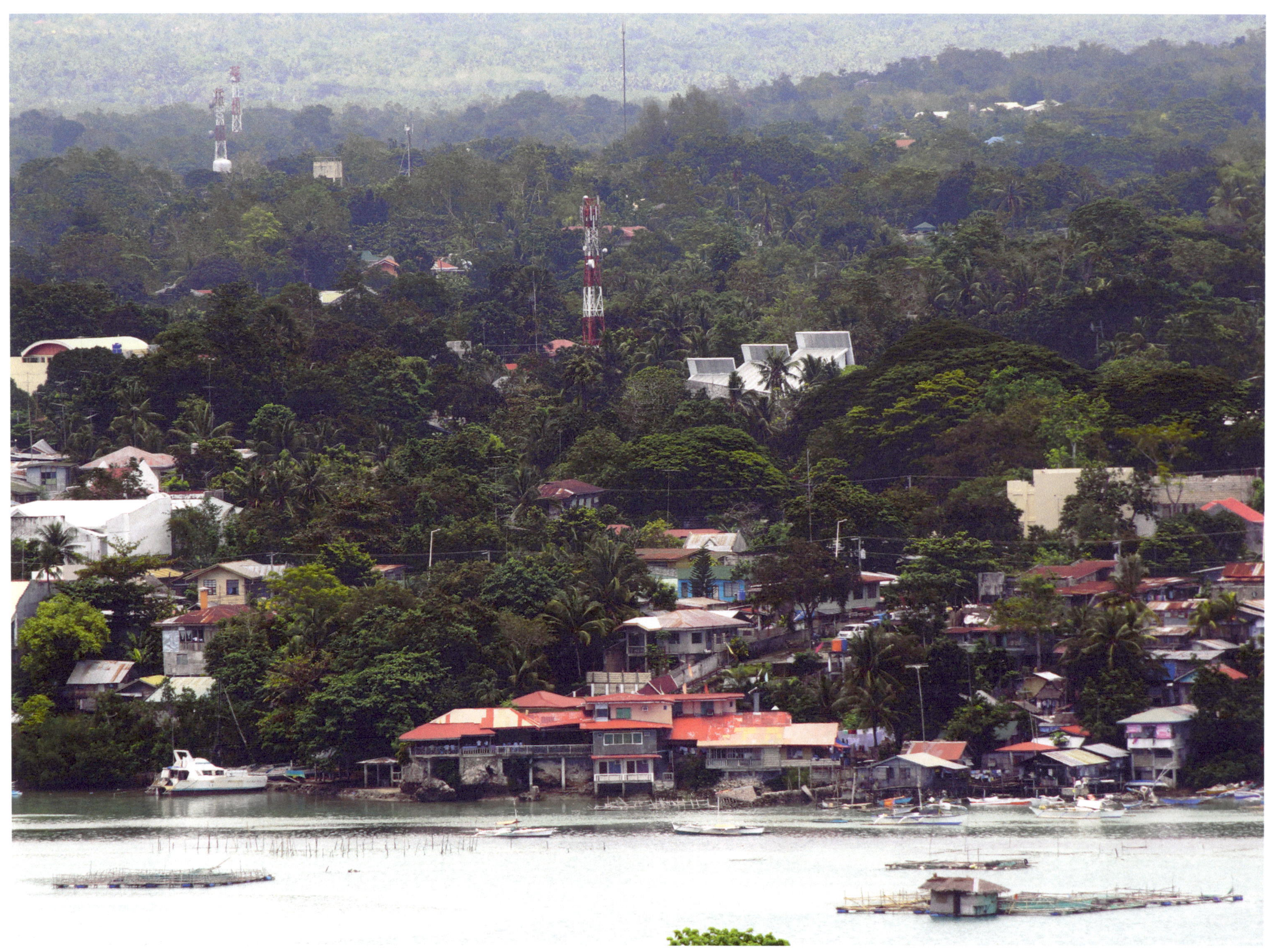

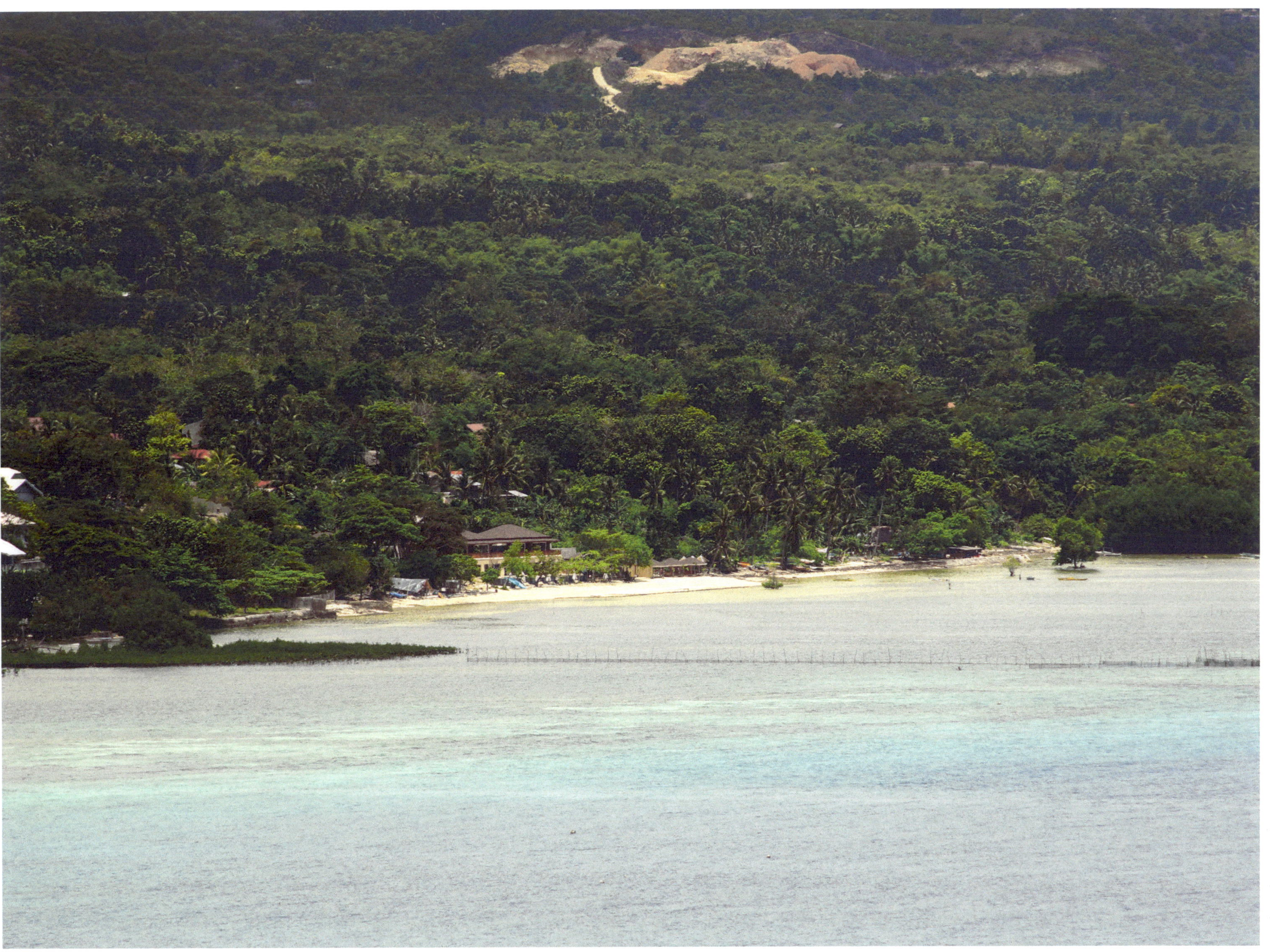

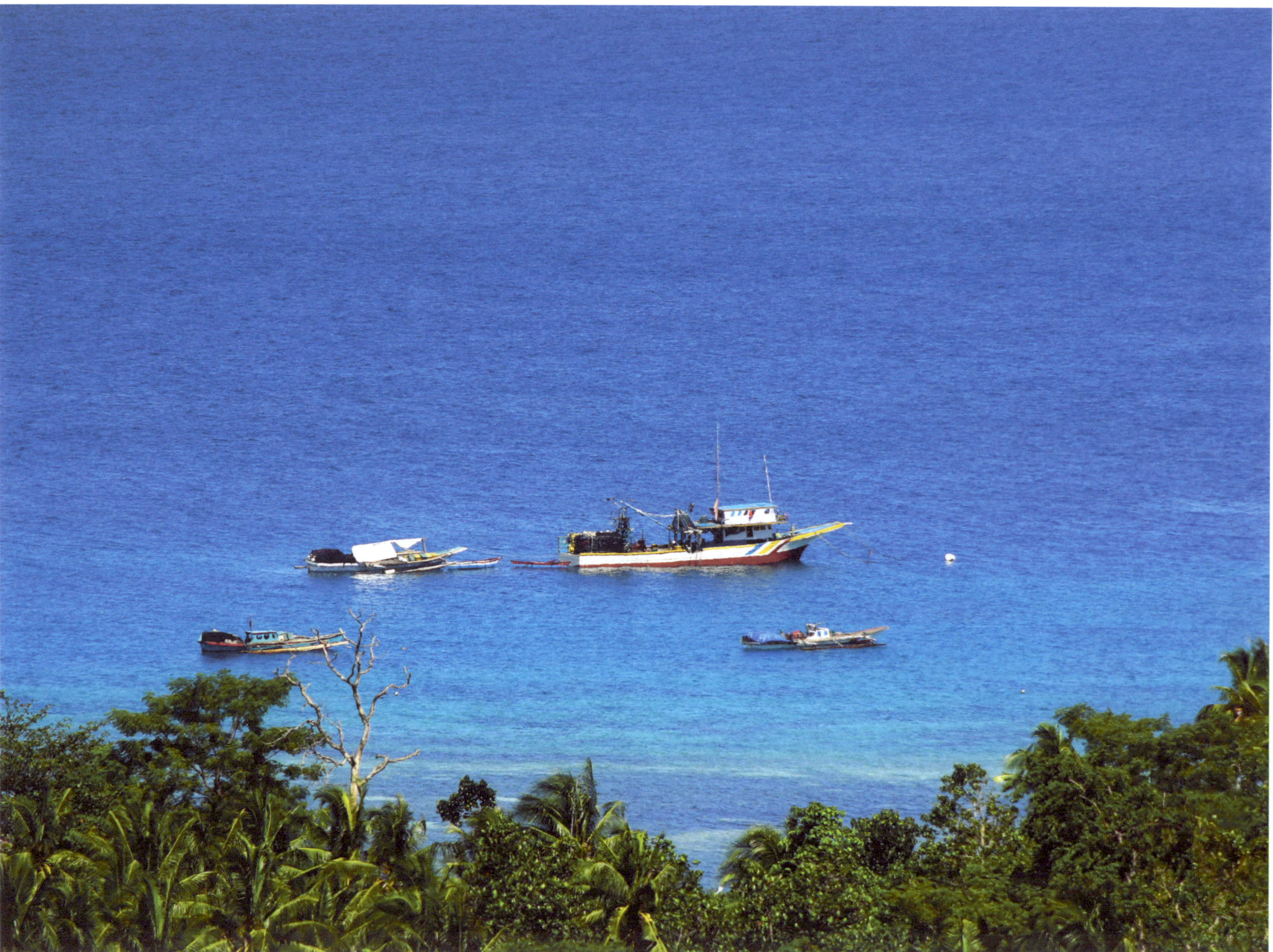

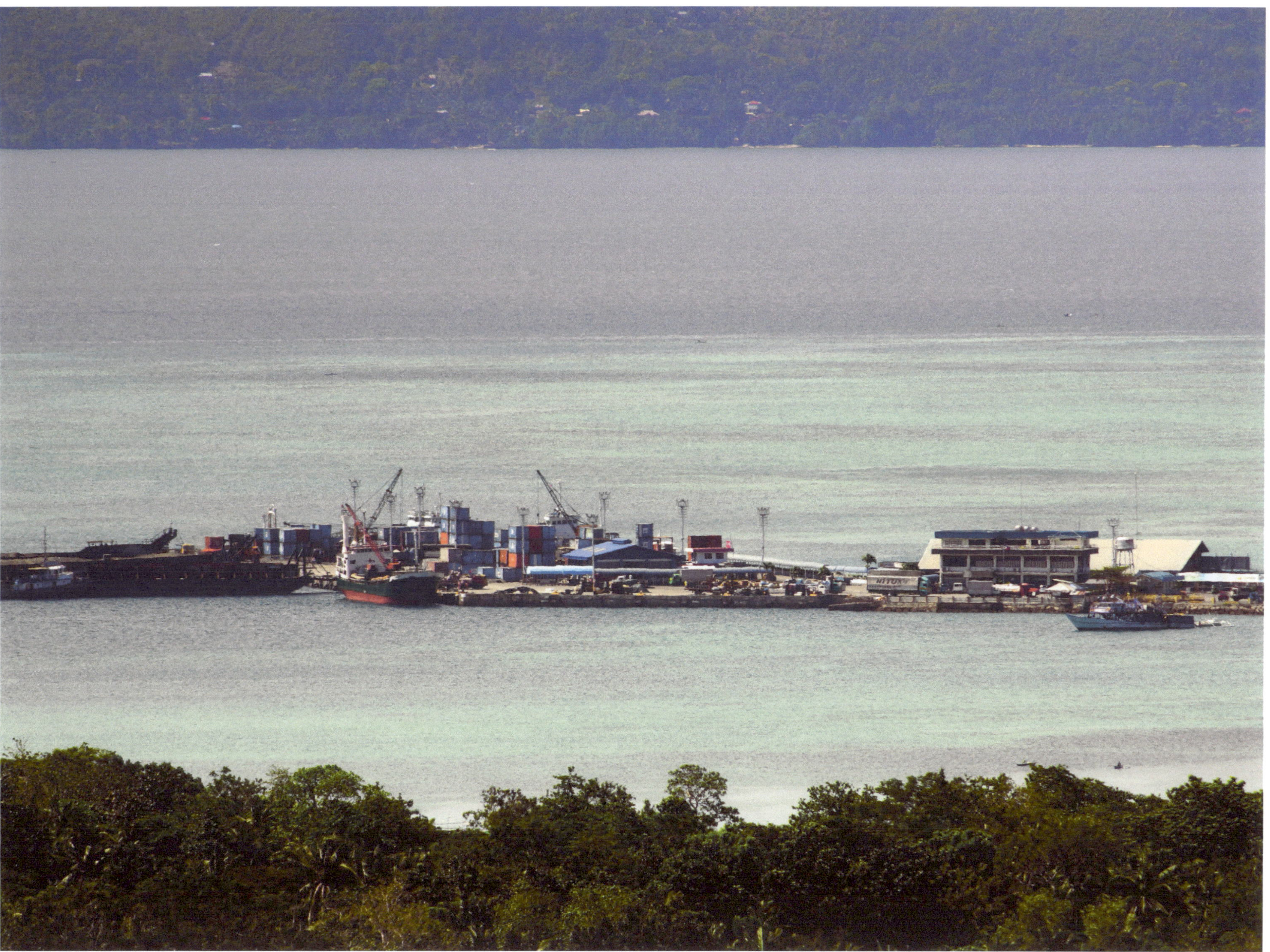

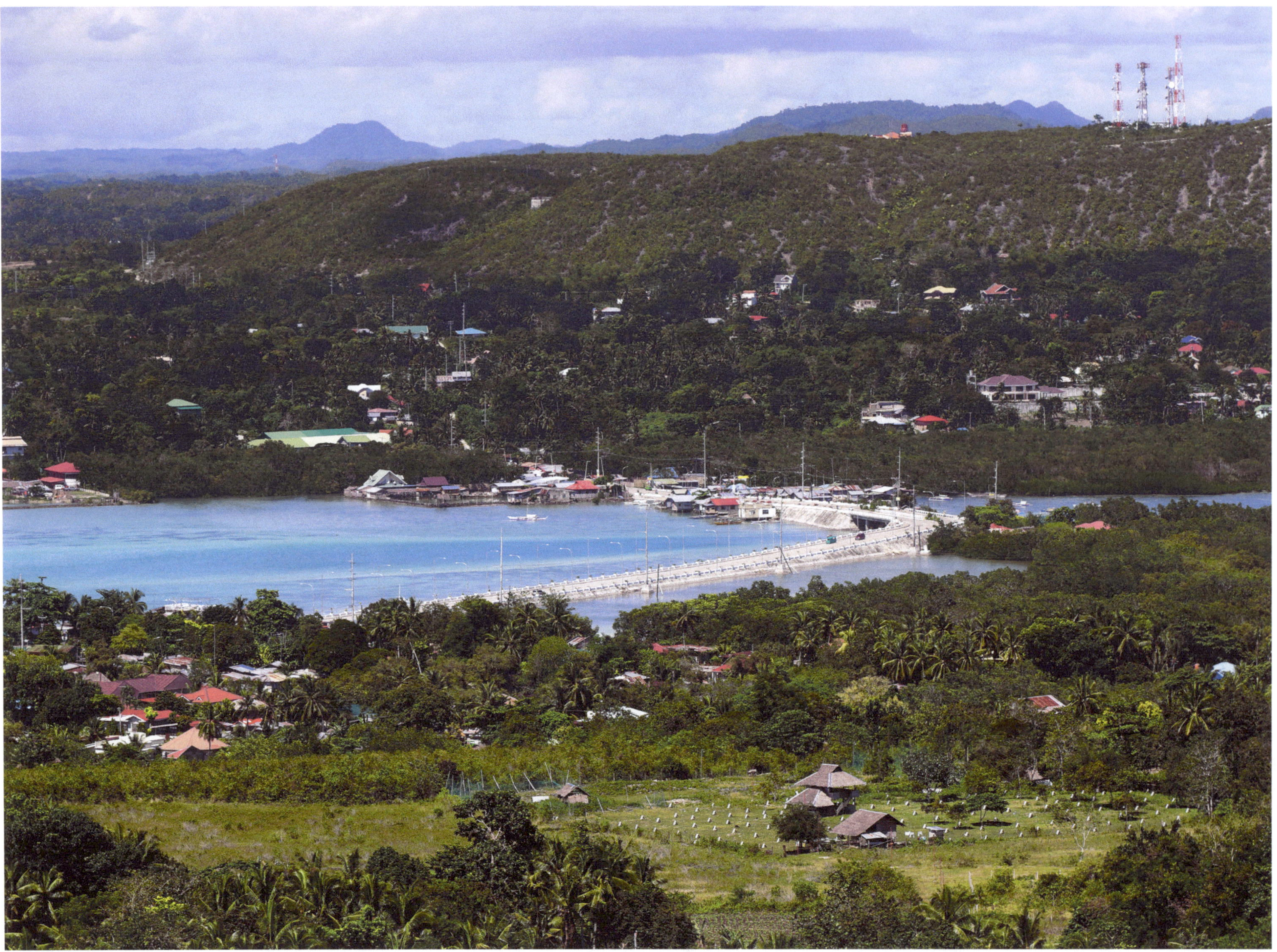

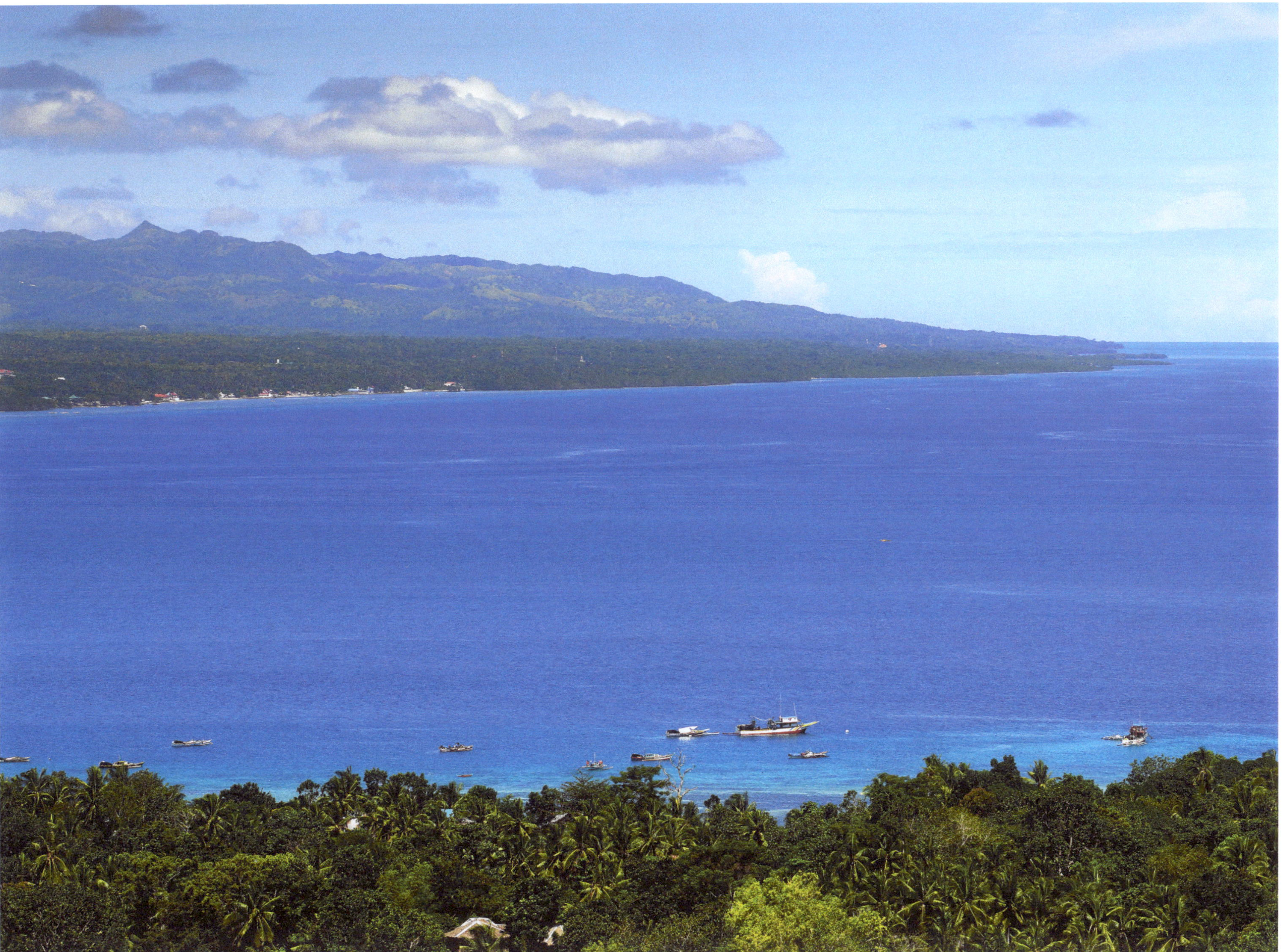

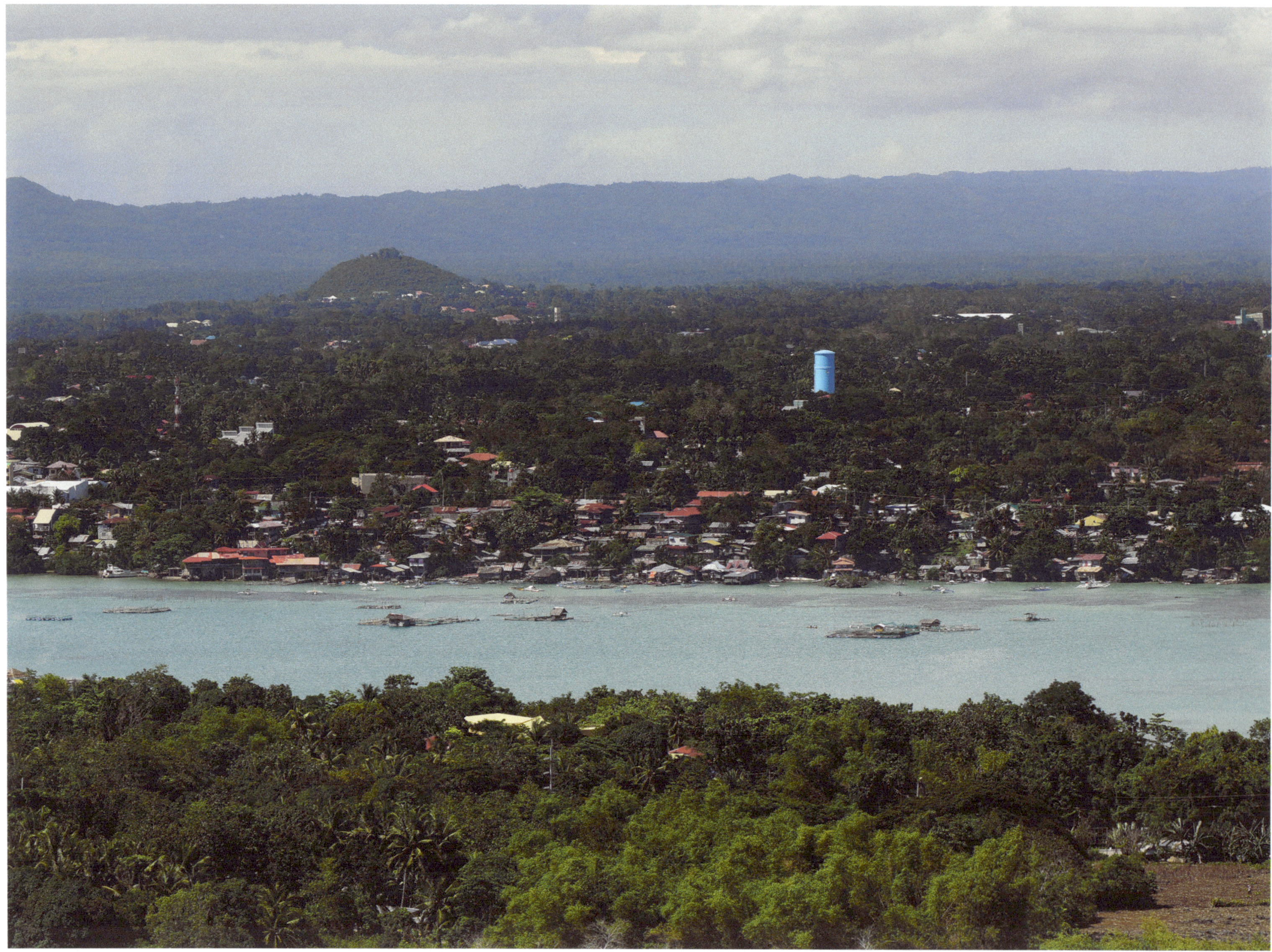

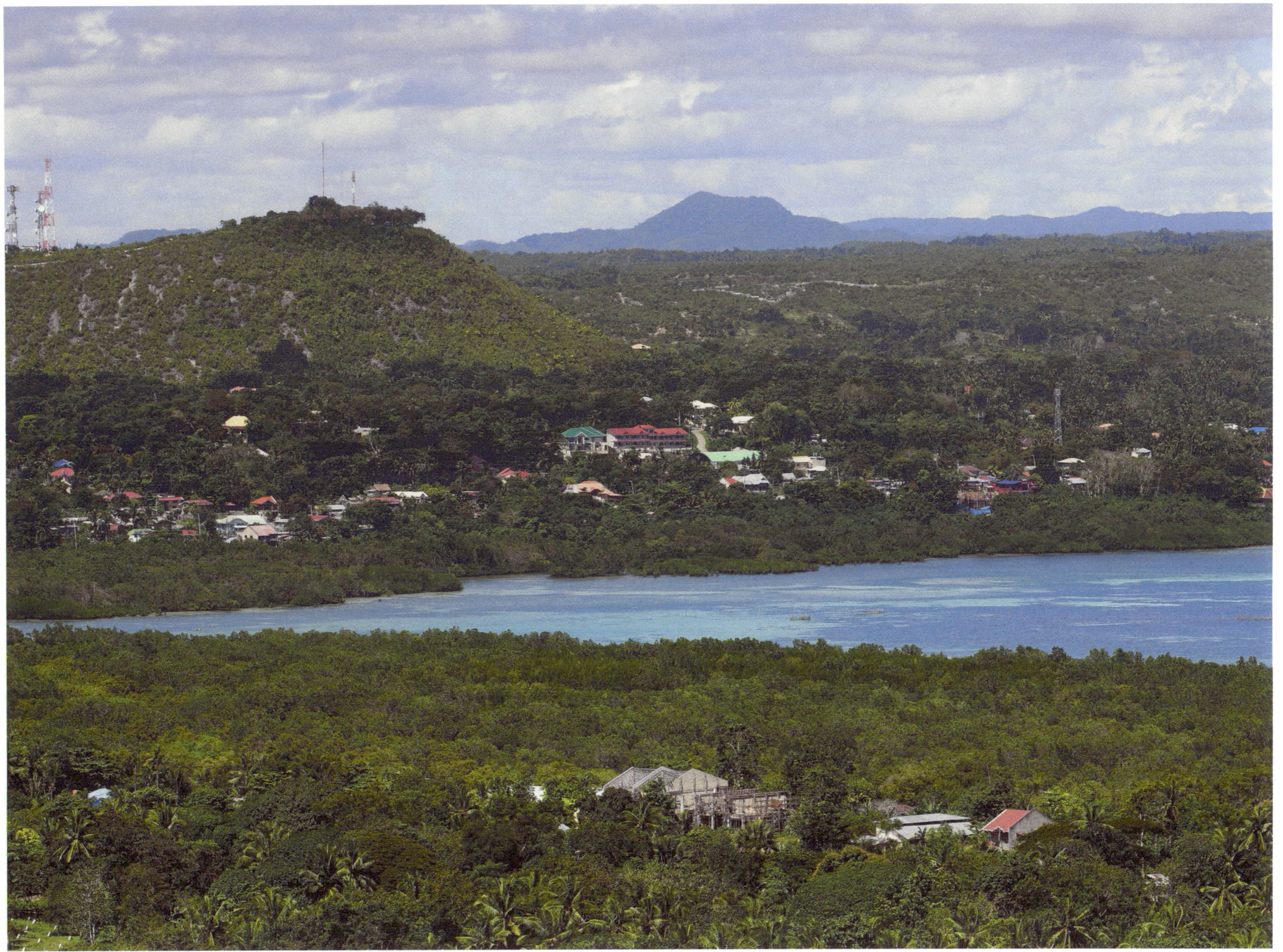

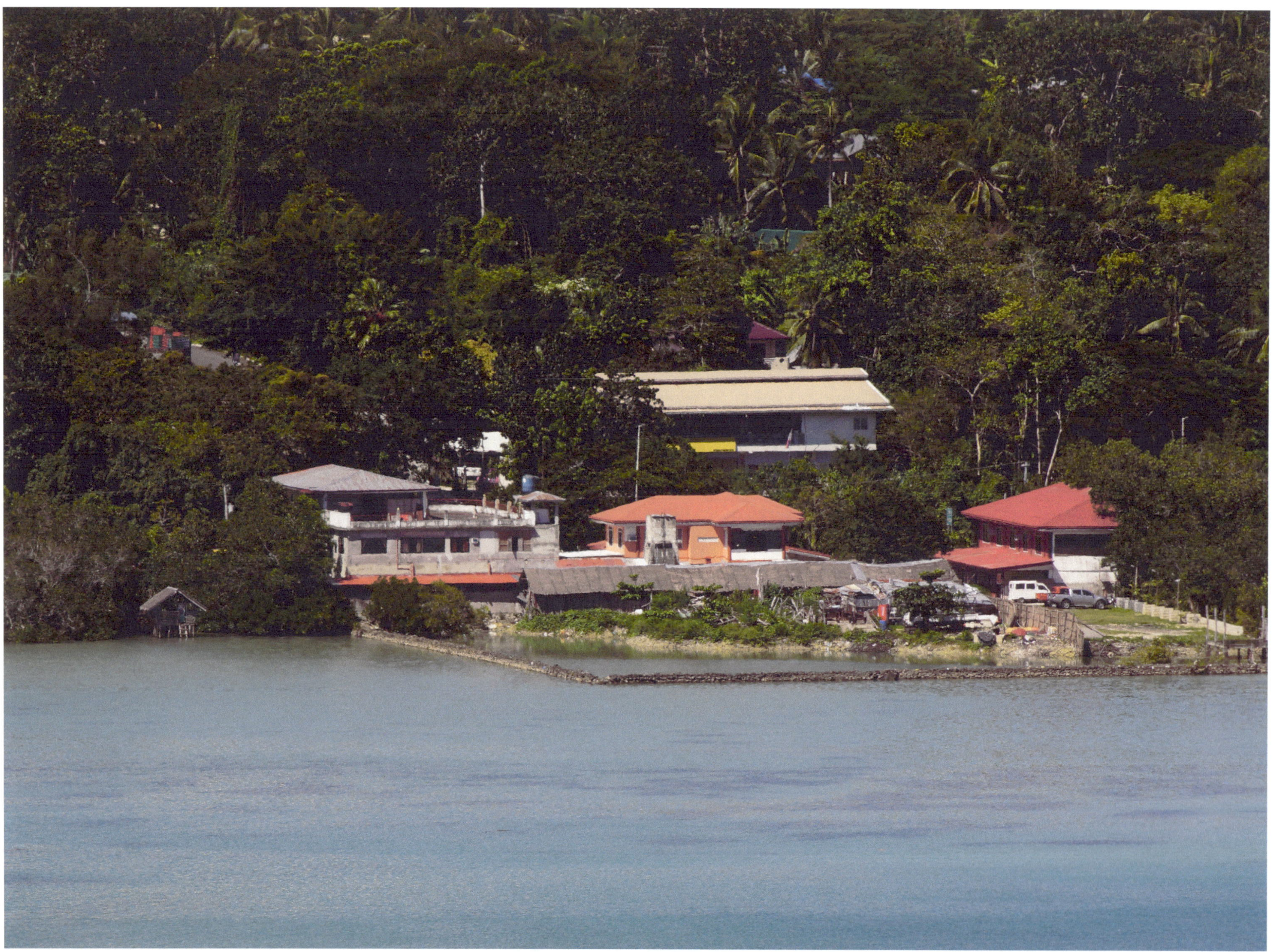

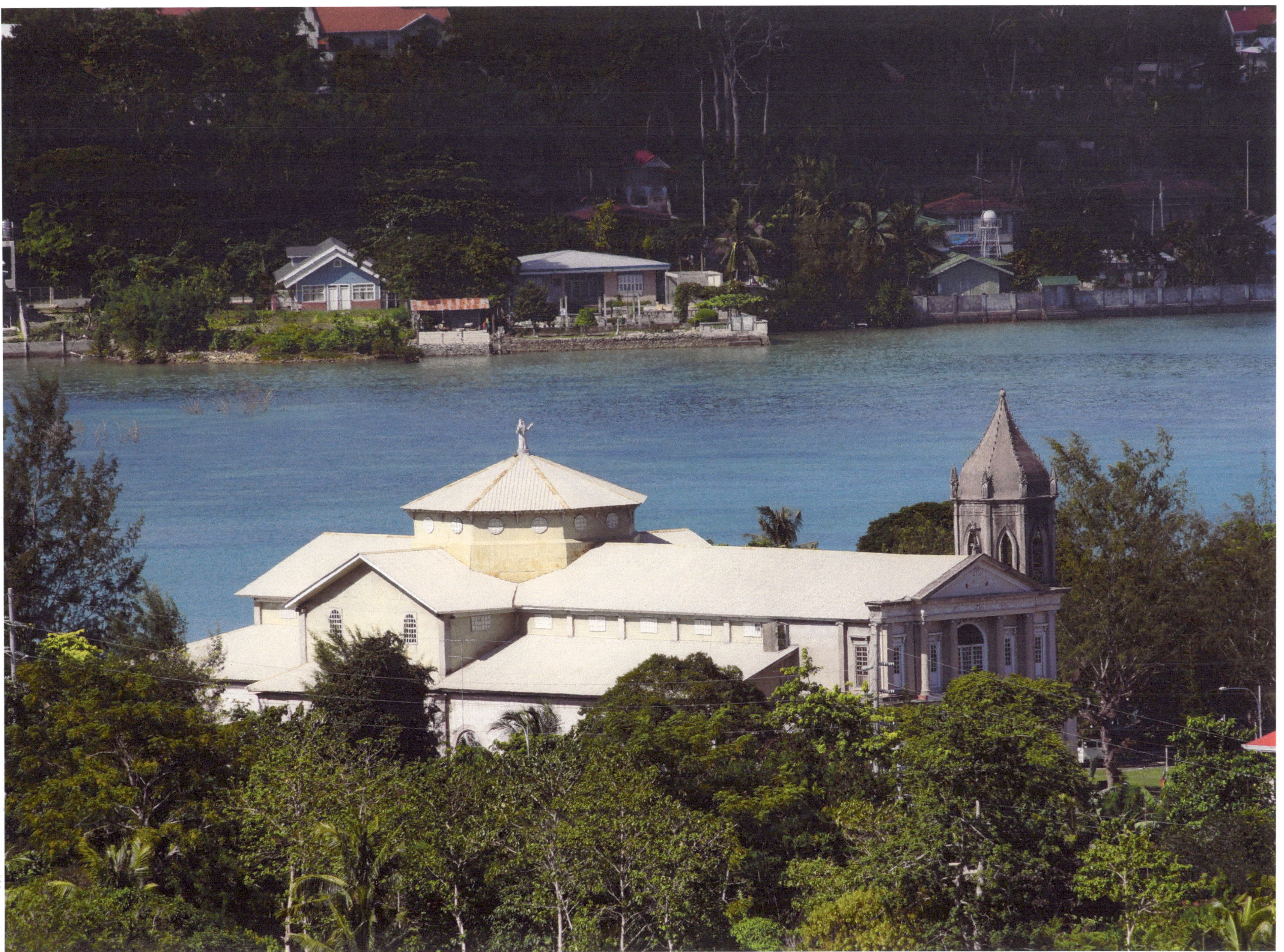

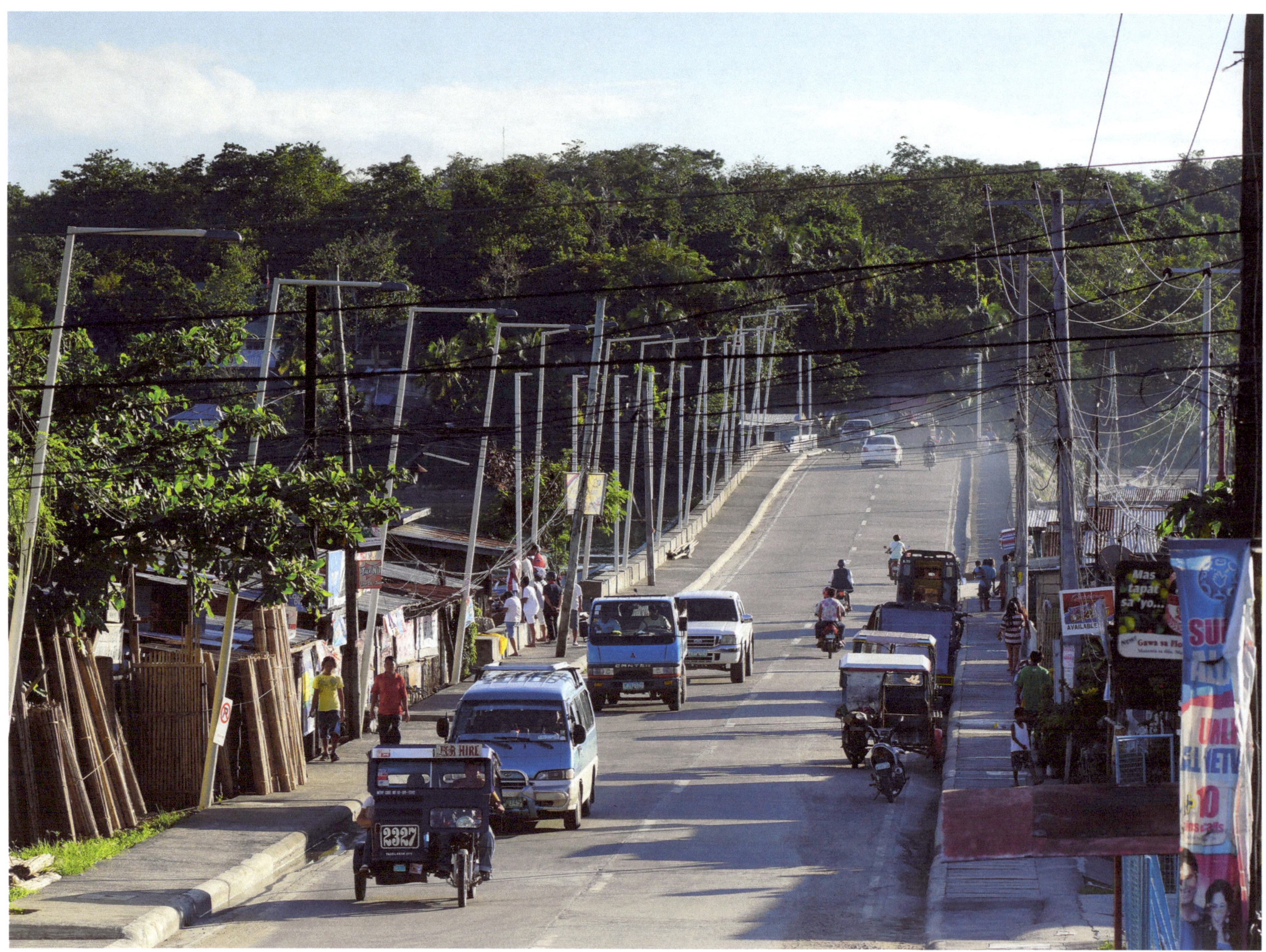
HIRE
2327
CANTER
AVAILABLE

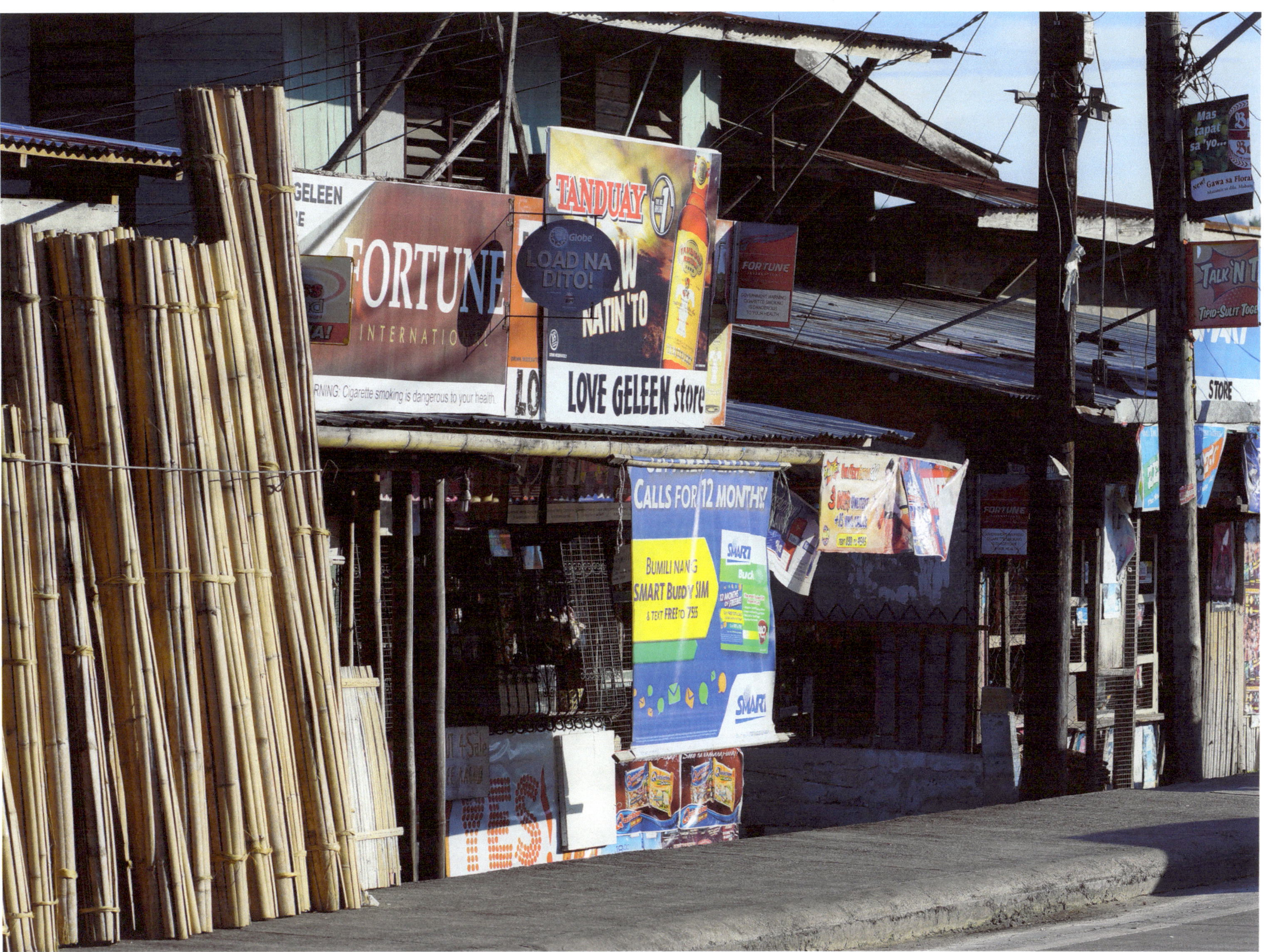

GELEEN
FORTUNE
Cigarette smoking is dangerous to your health.
TANDUAY
Globe
LOAD NA DITO!
NATIN'TO
LOVE GELEEN store
FORTUNE
Mas tapat sa'yo...
STORE
CALLS FOR 12 MONTHS!
BUMILI NANG
SMART Buddy SIM
SMART
YES!

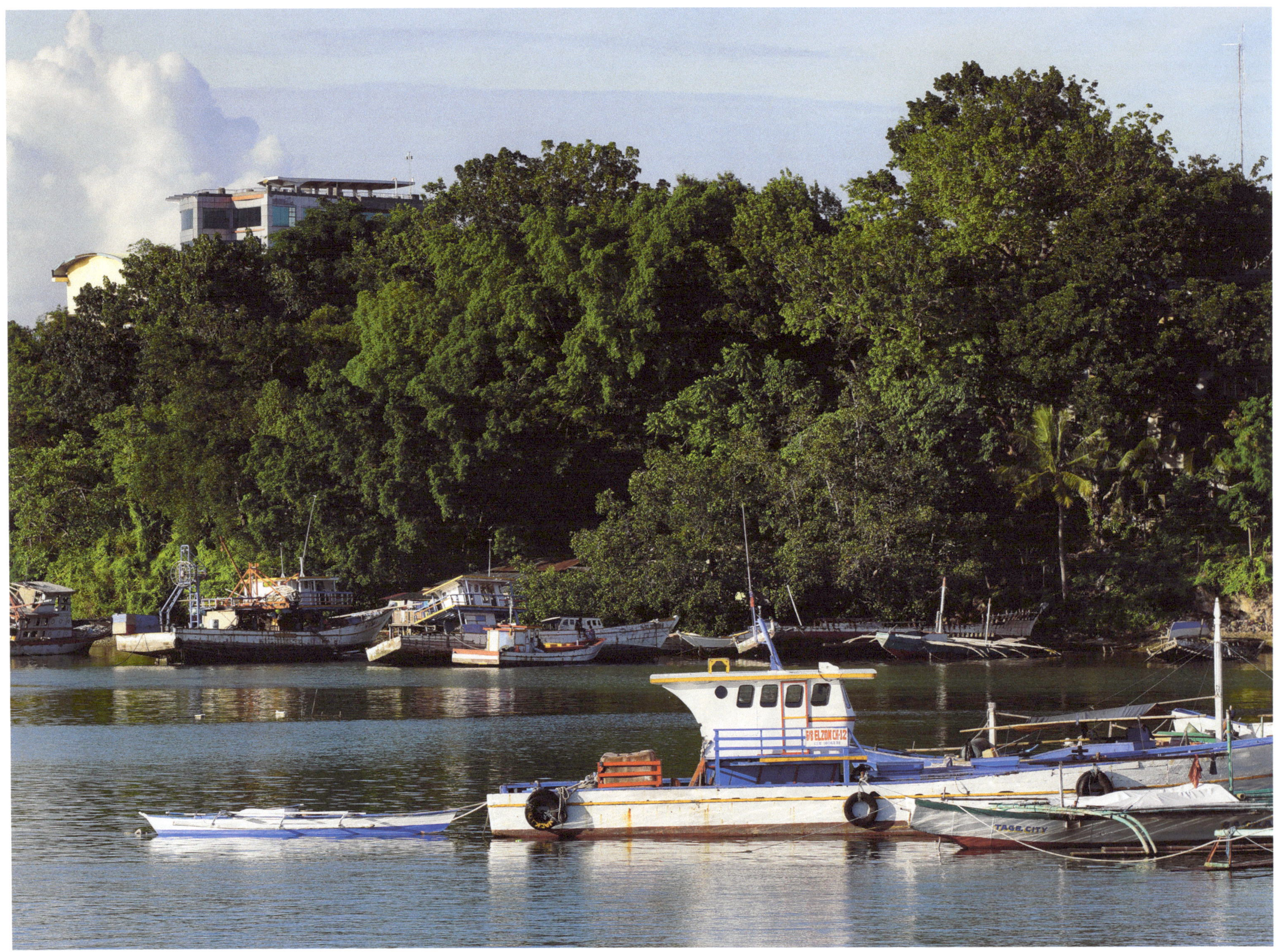
F/B ELZON CH-12
TAGB.CITY

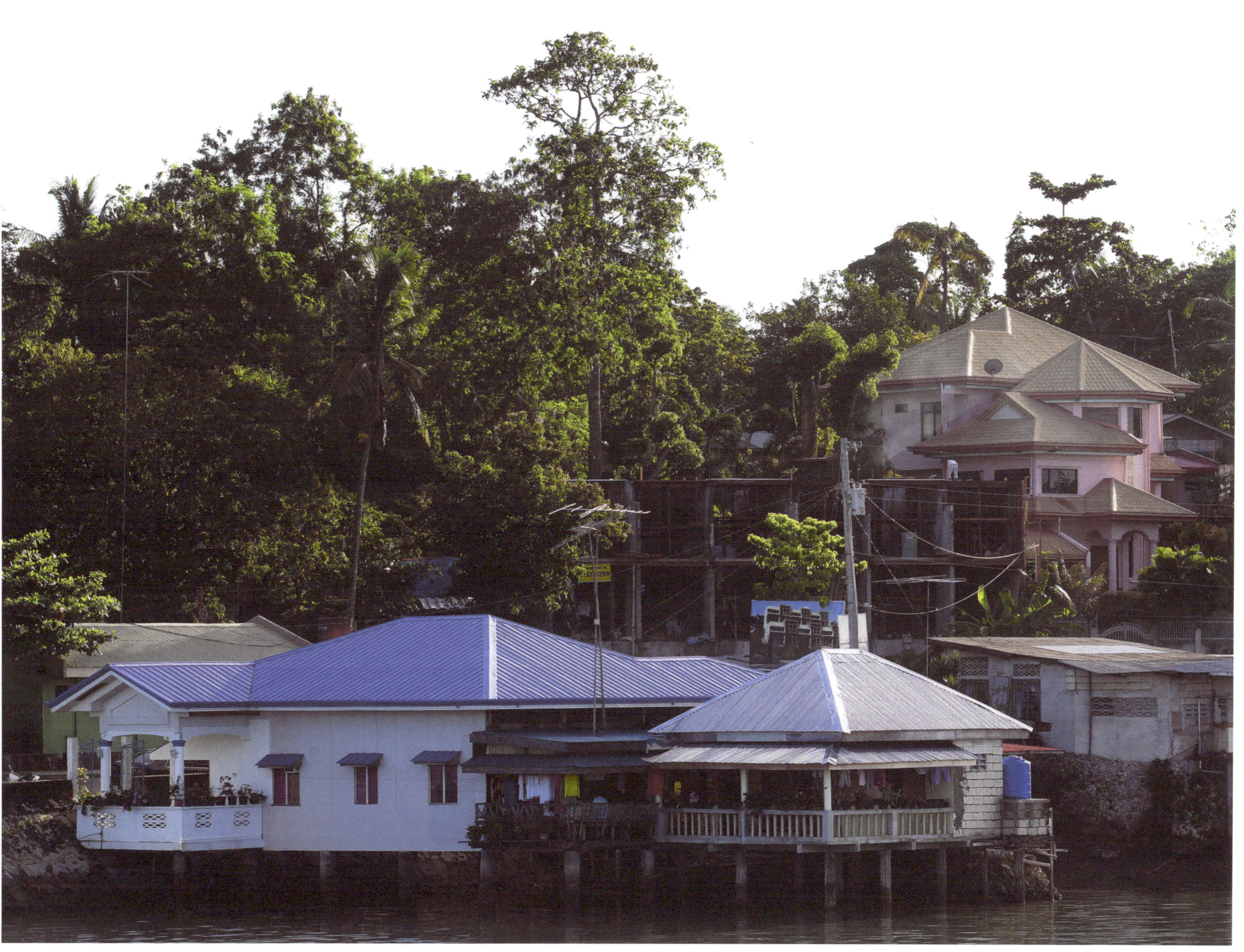

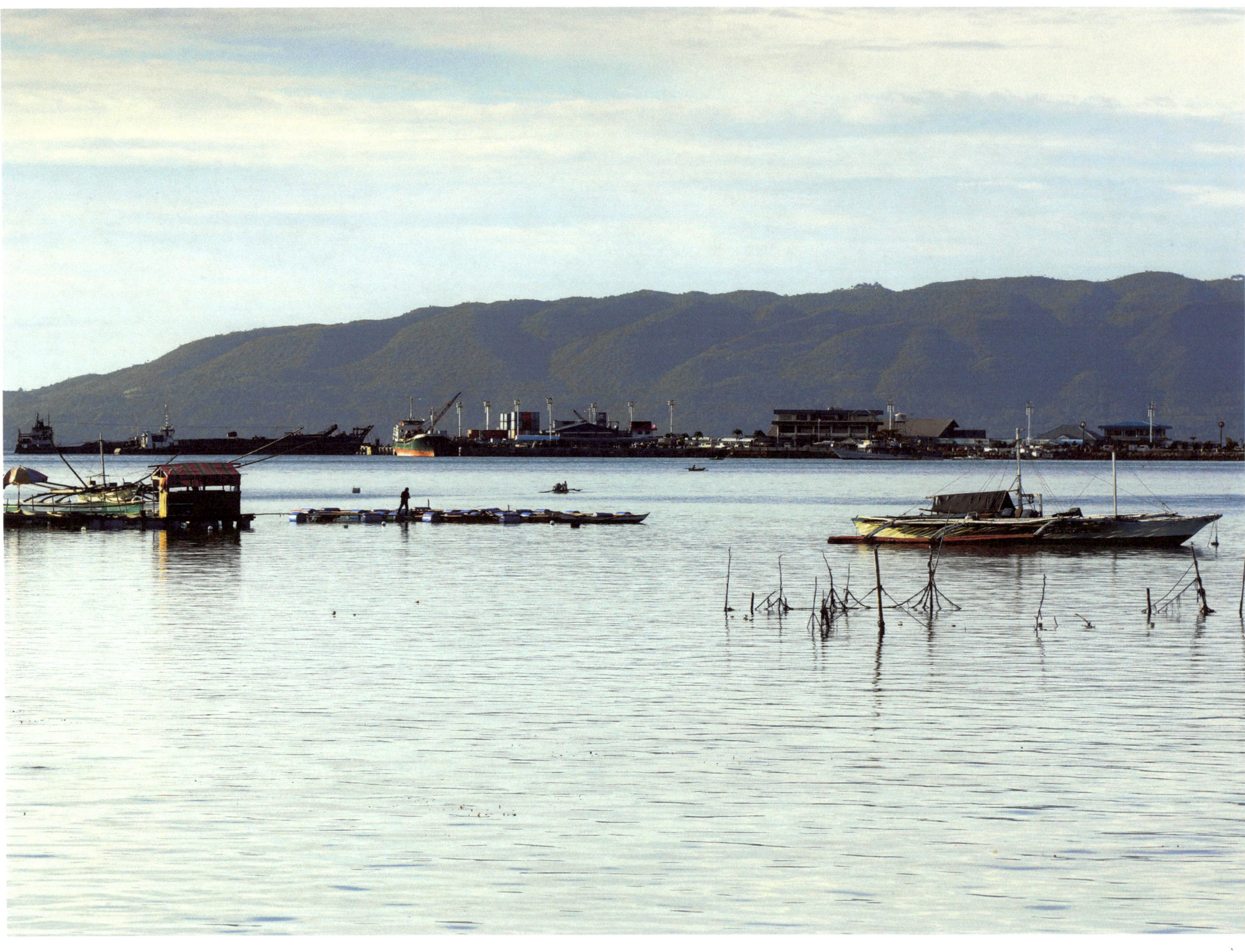

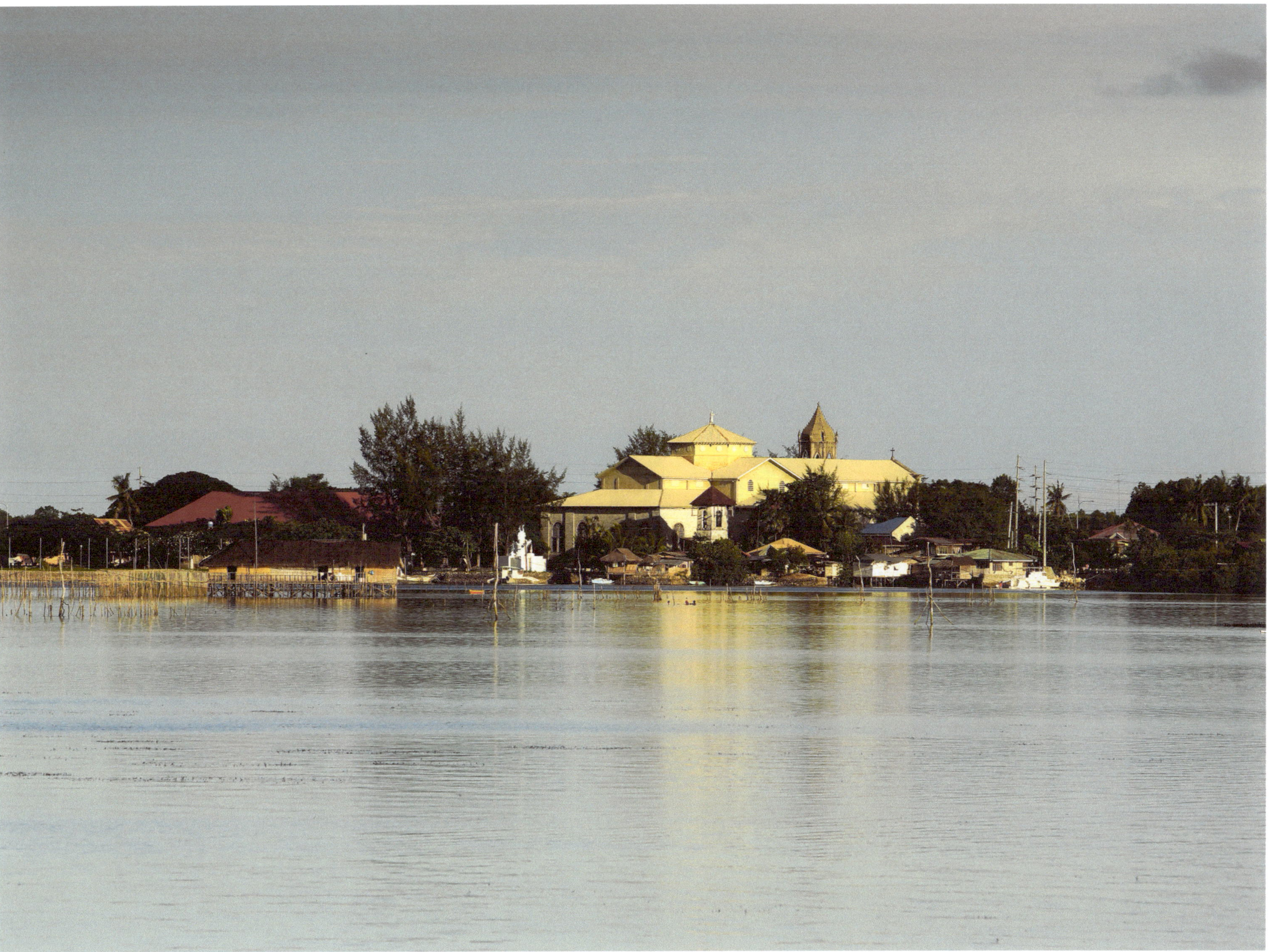

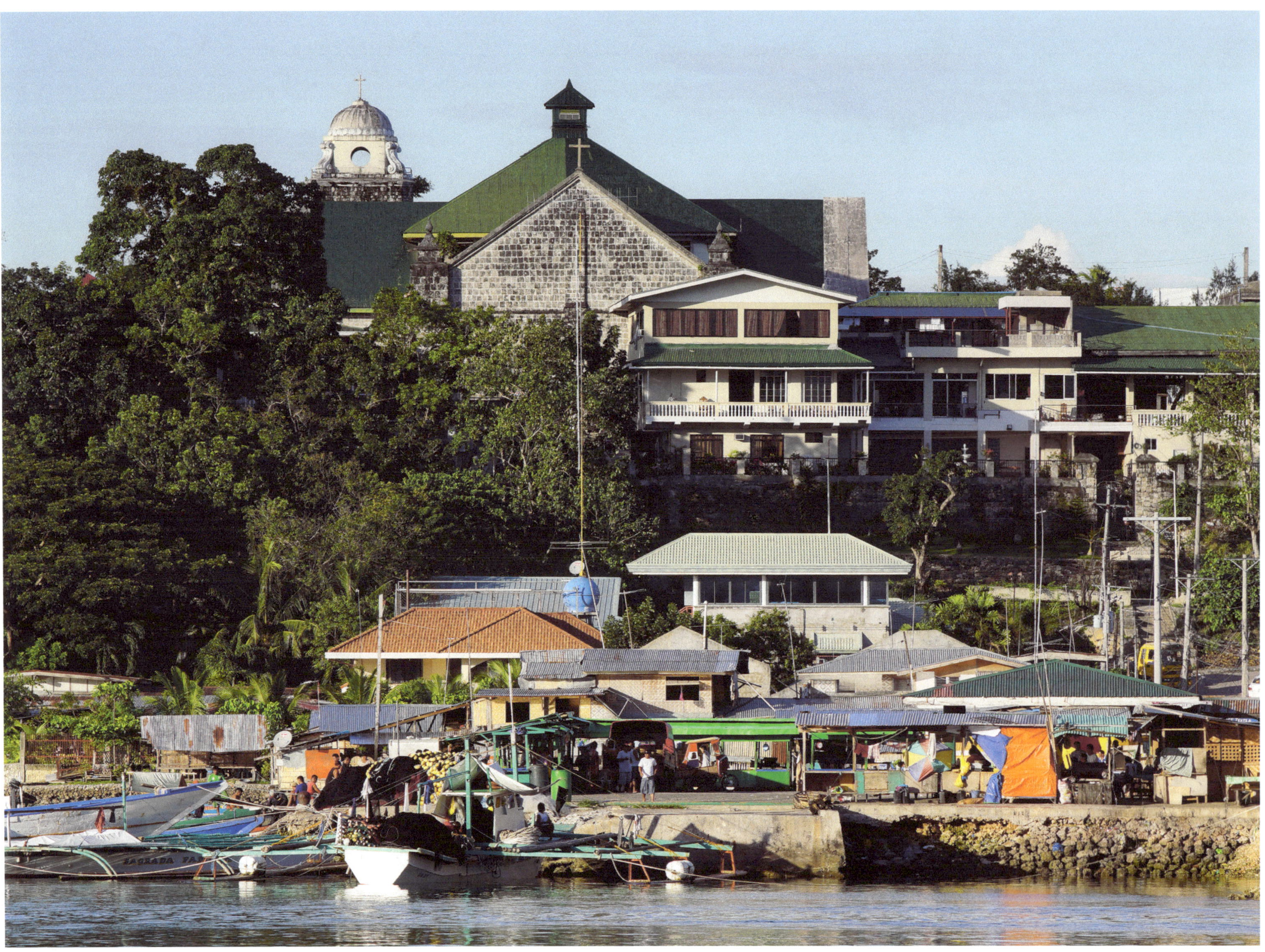

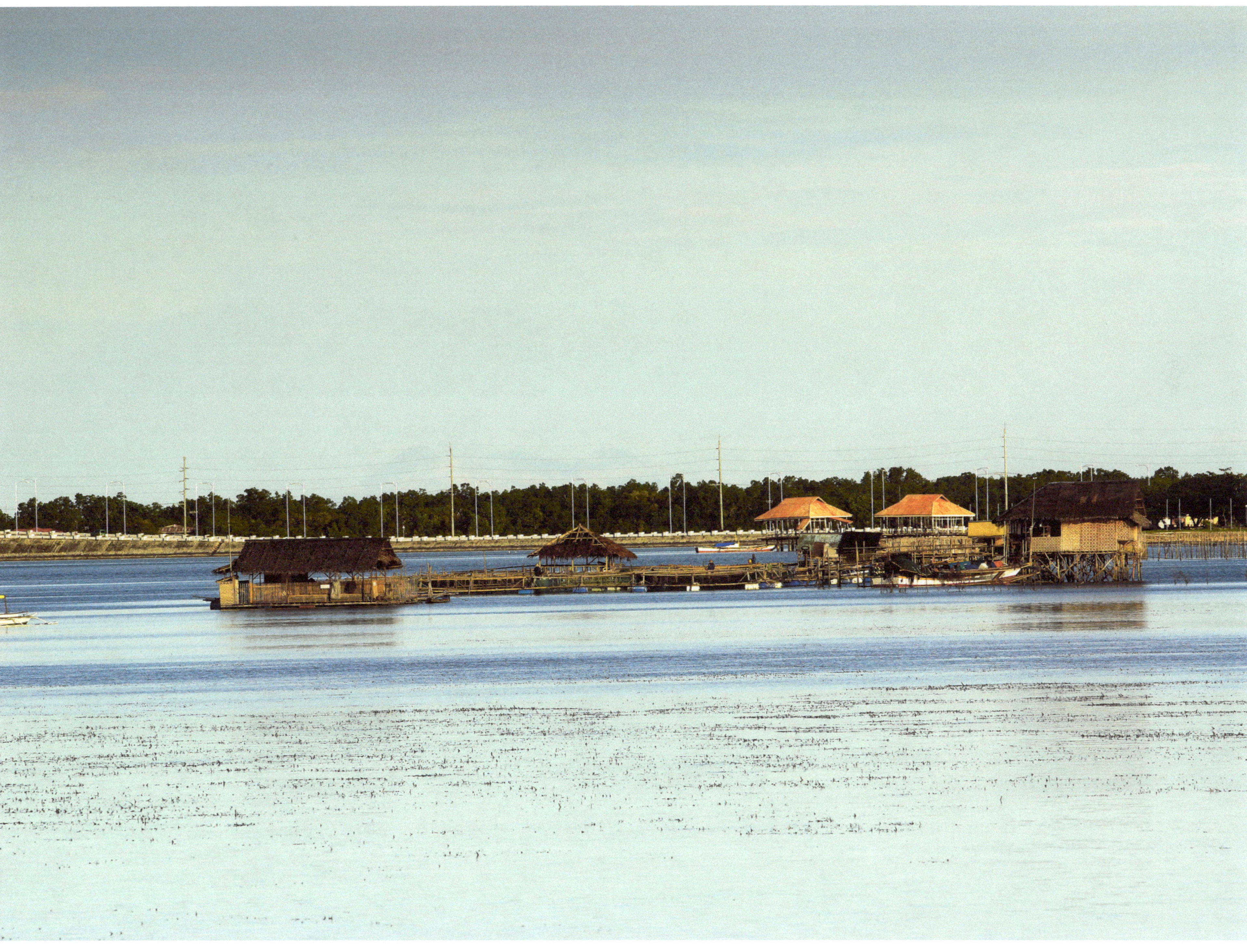

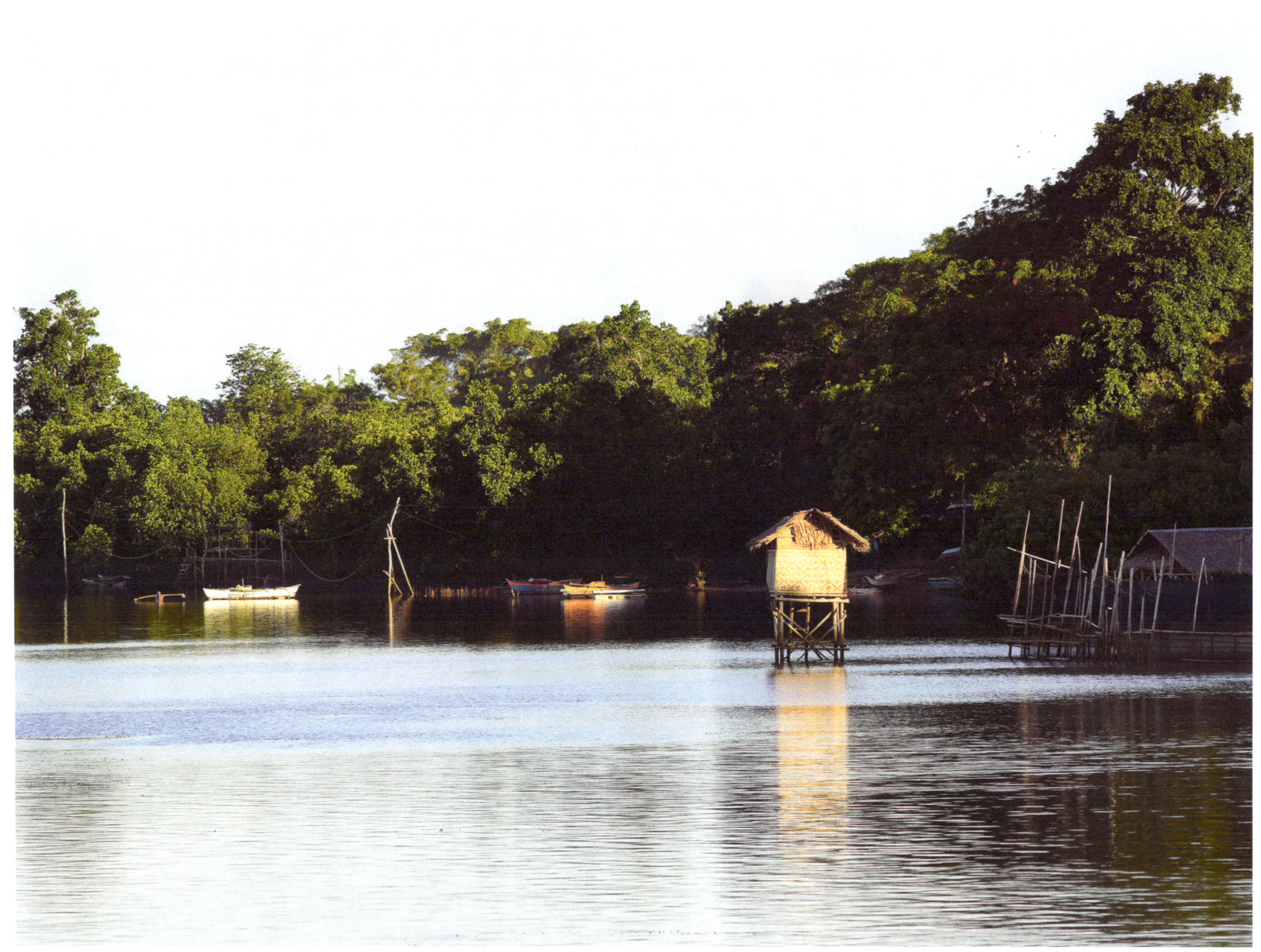

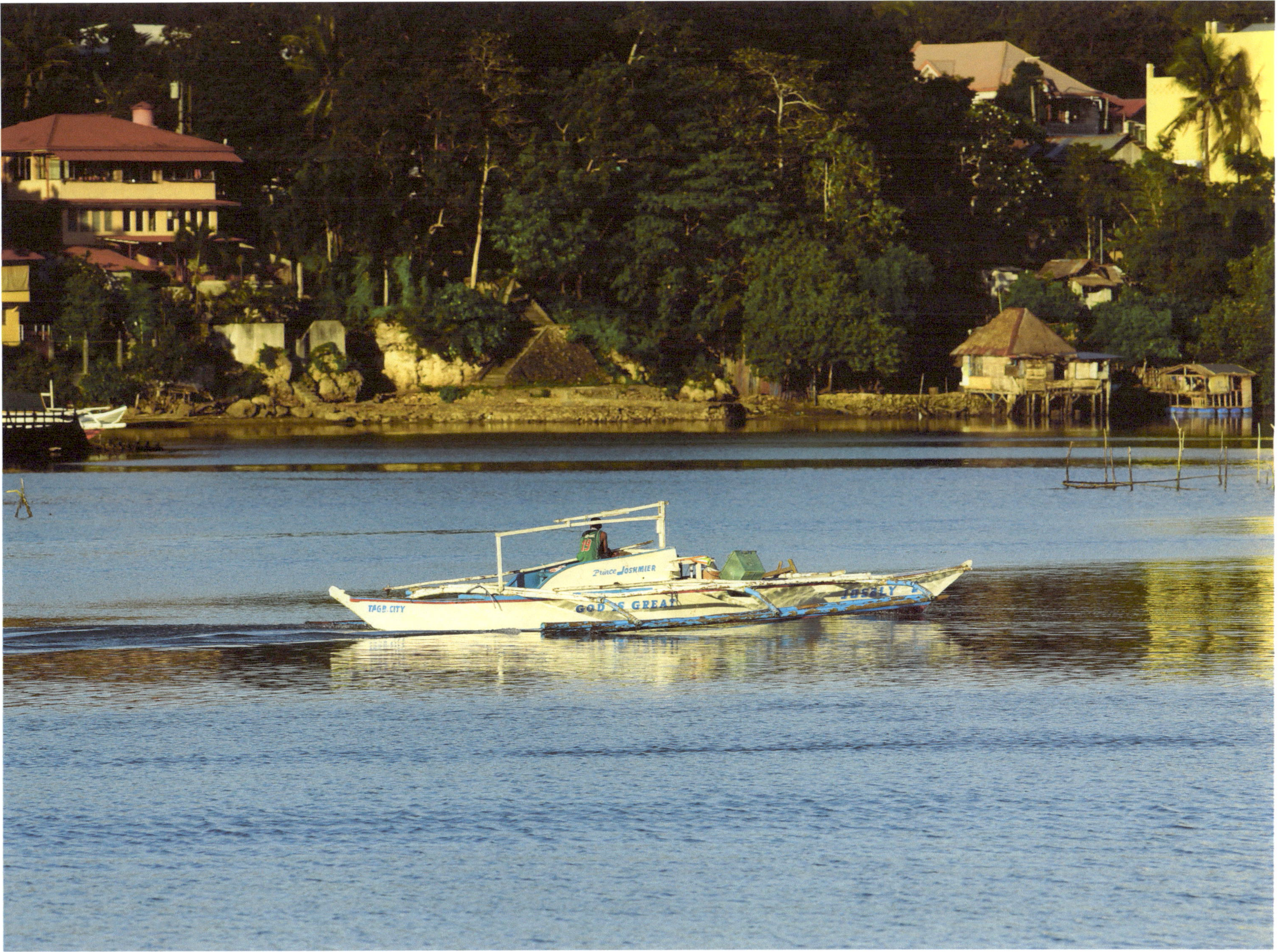
Prince JOSHMIER
TAGB. CITY

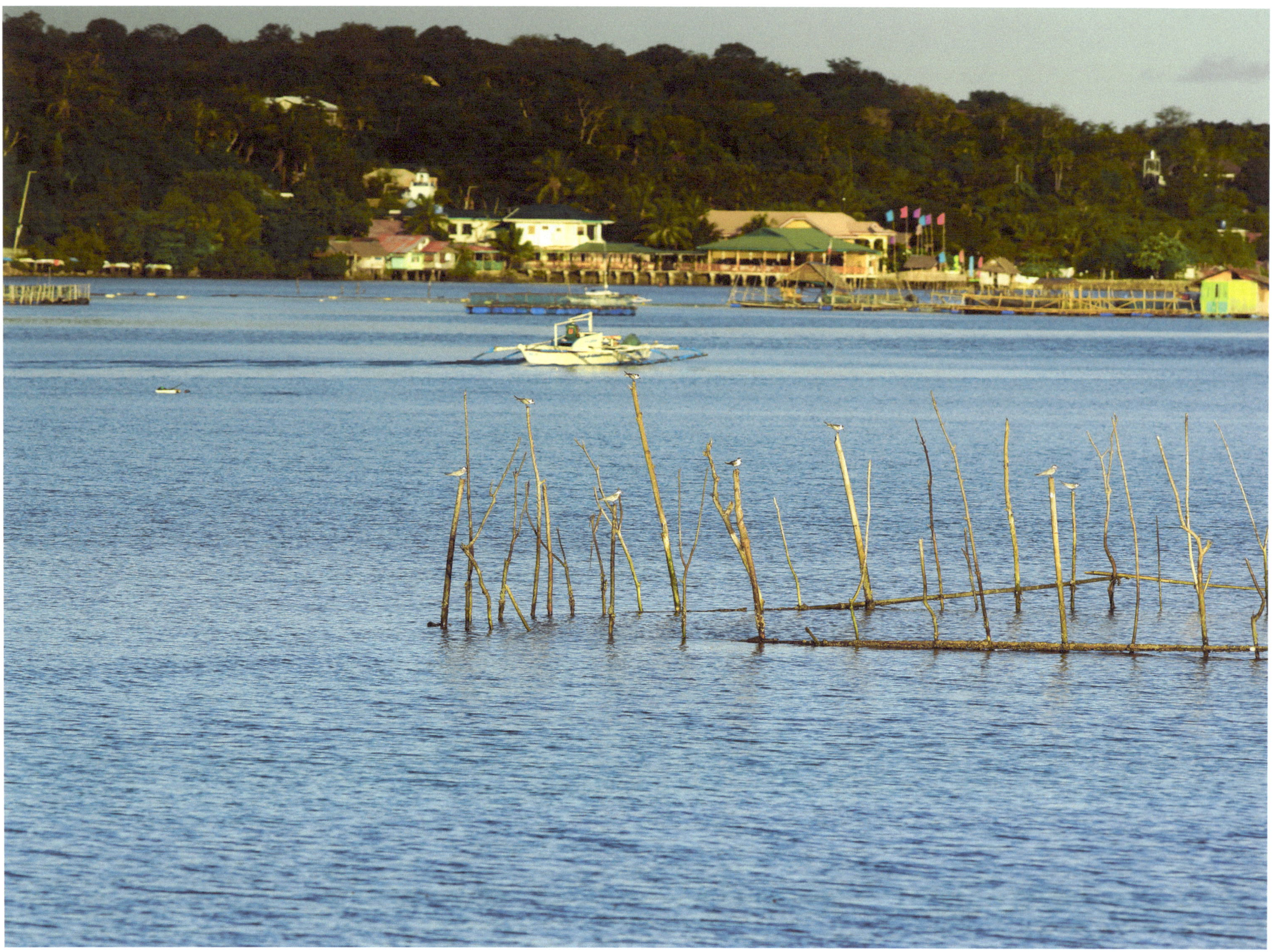

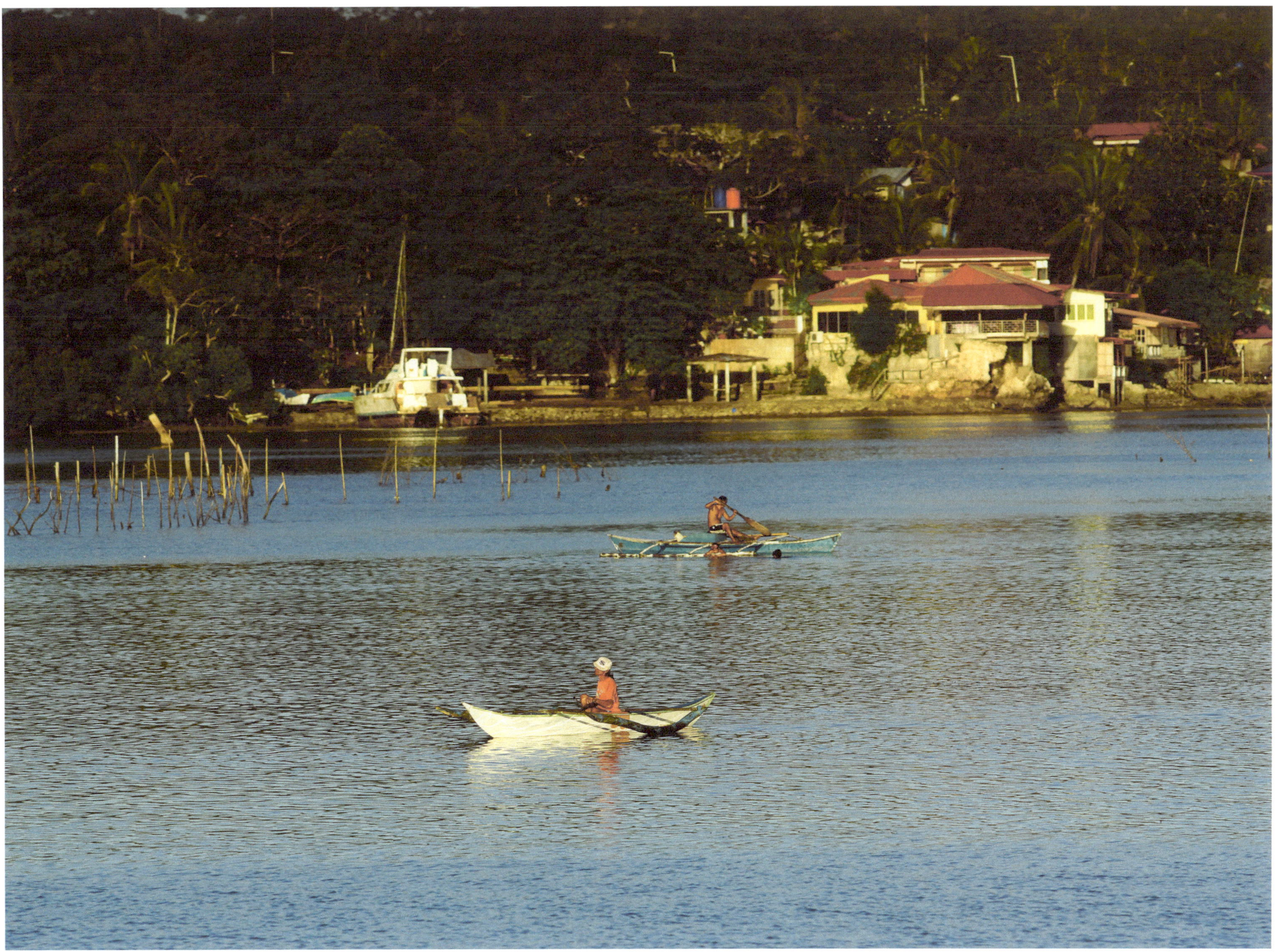

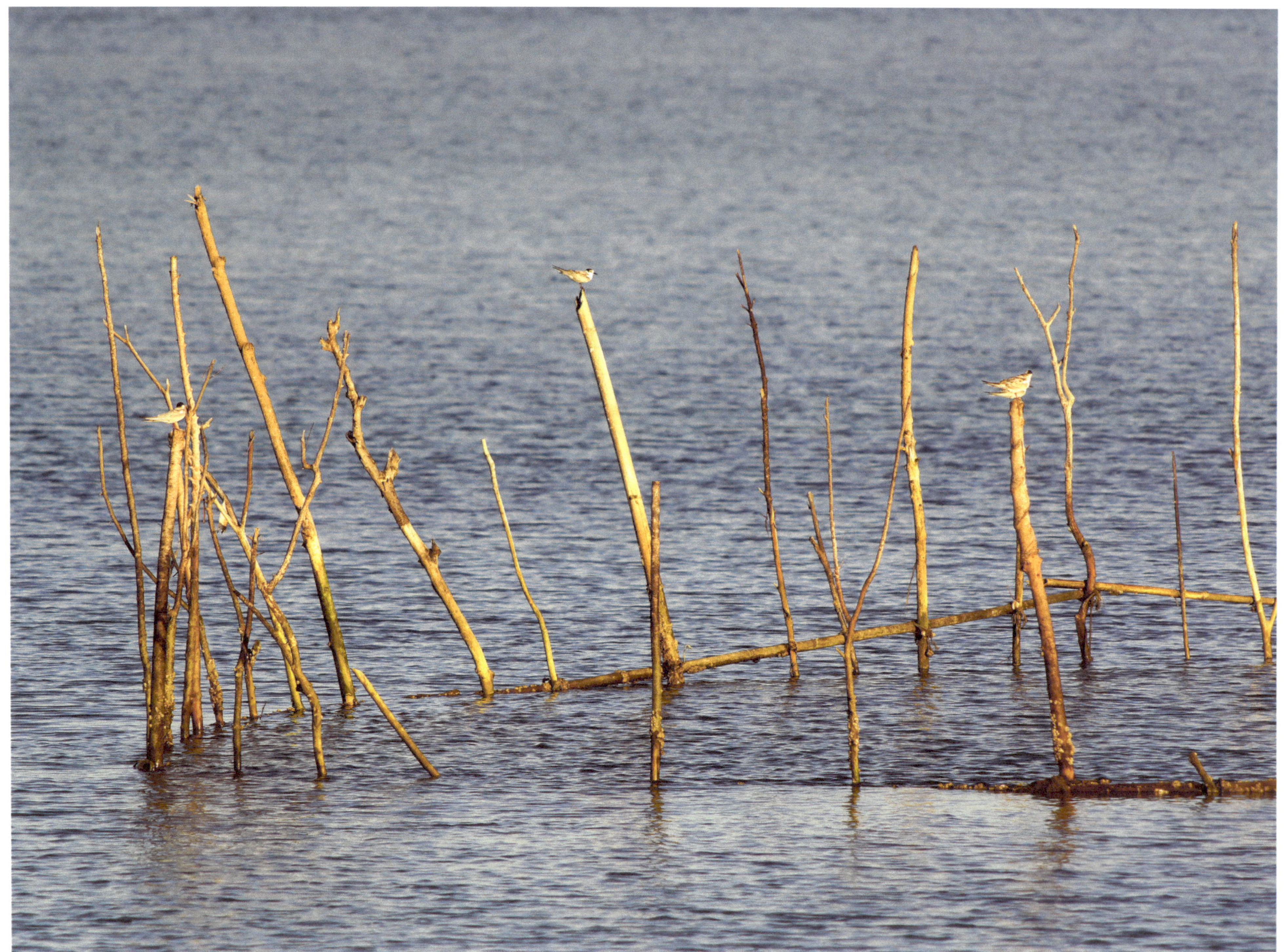

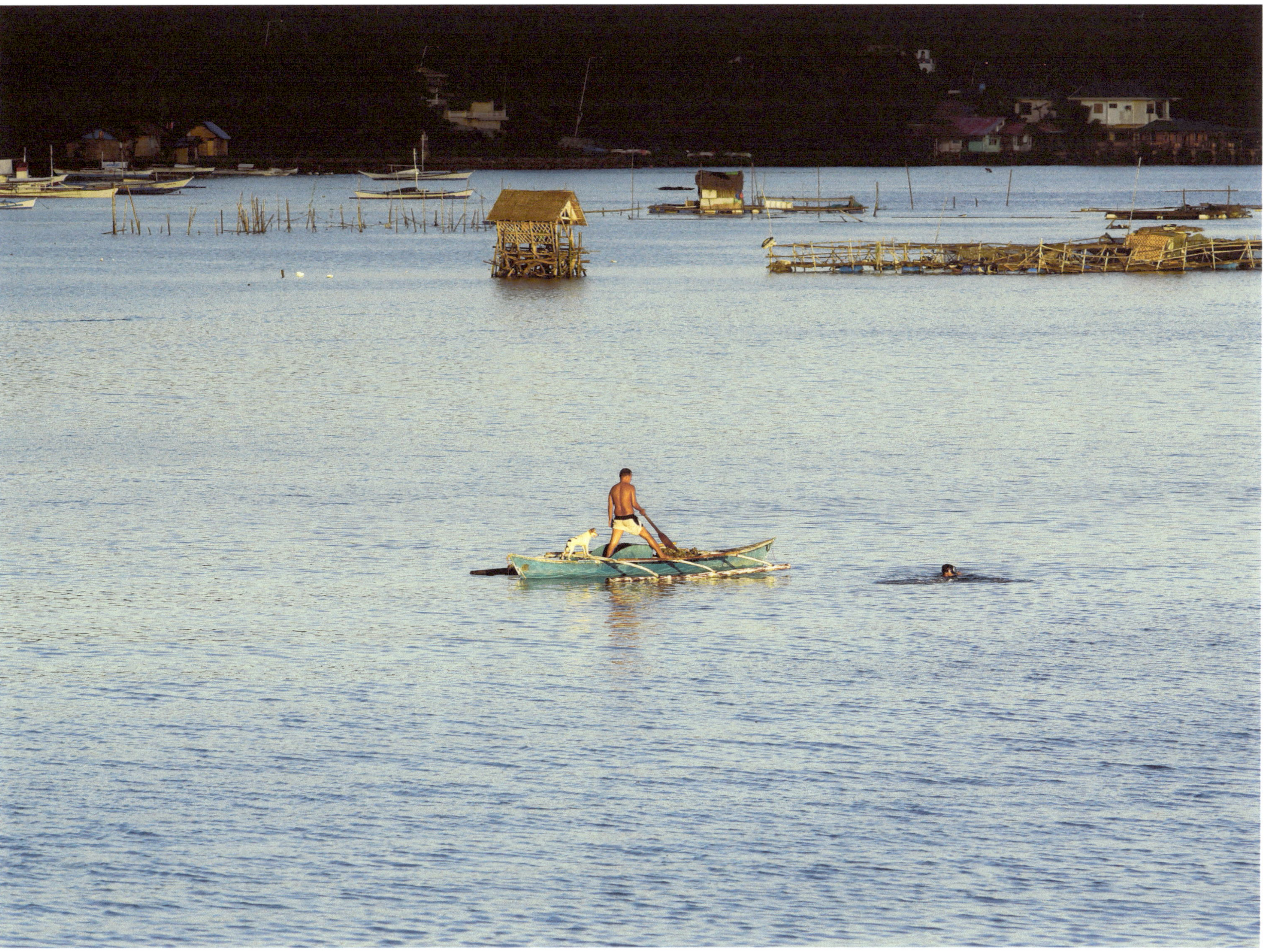

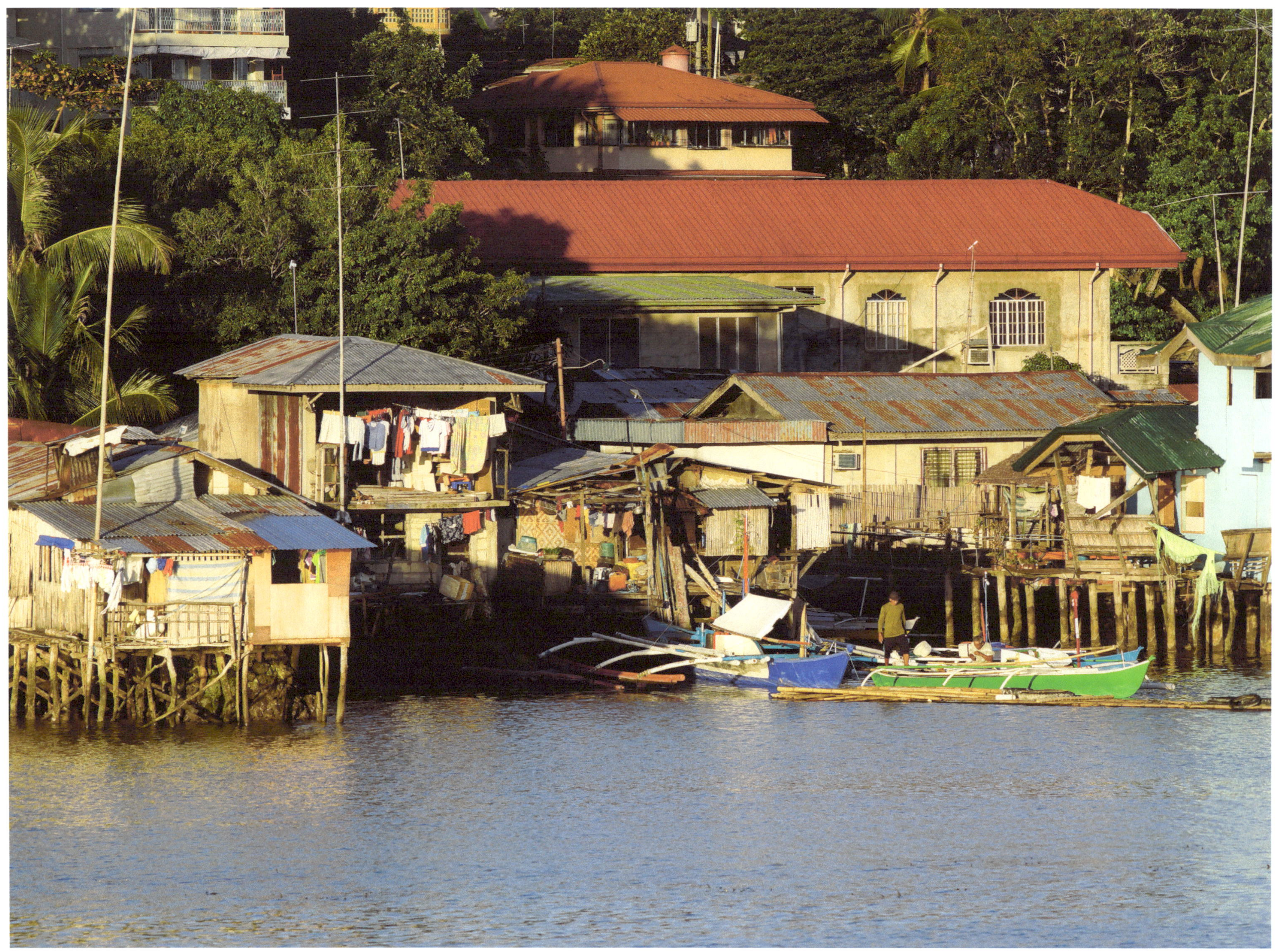

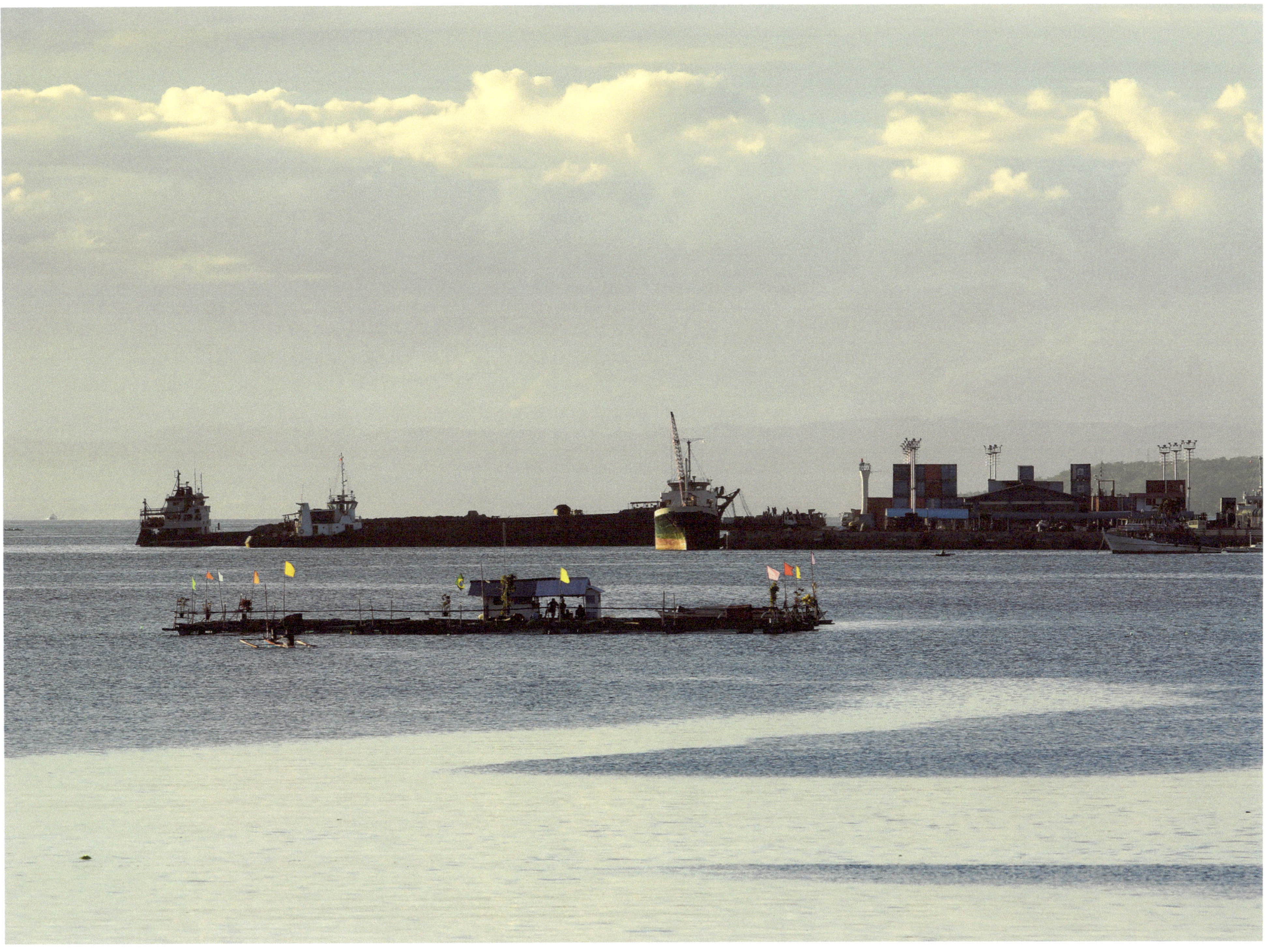

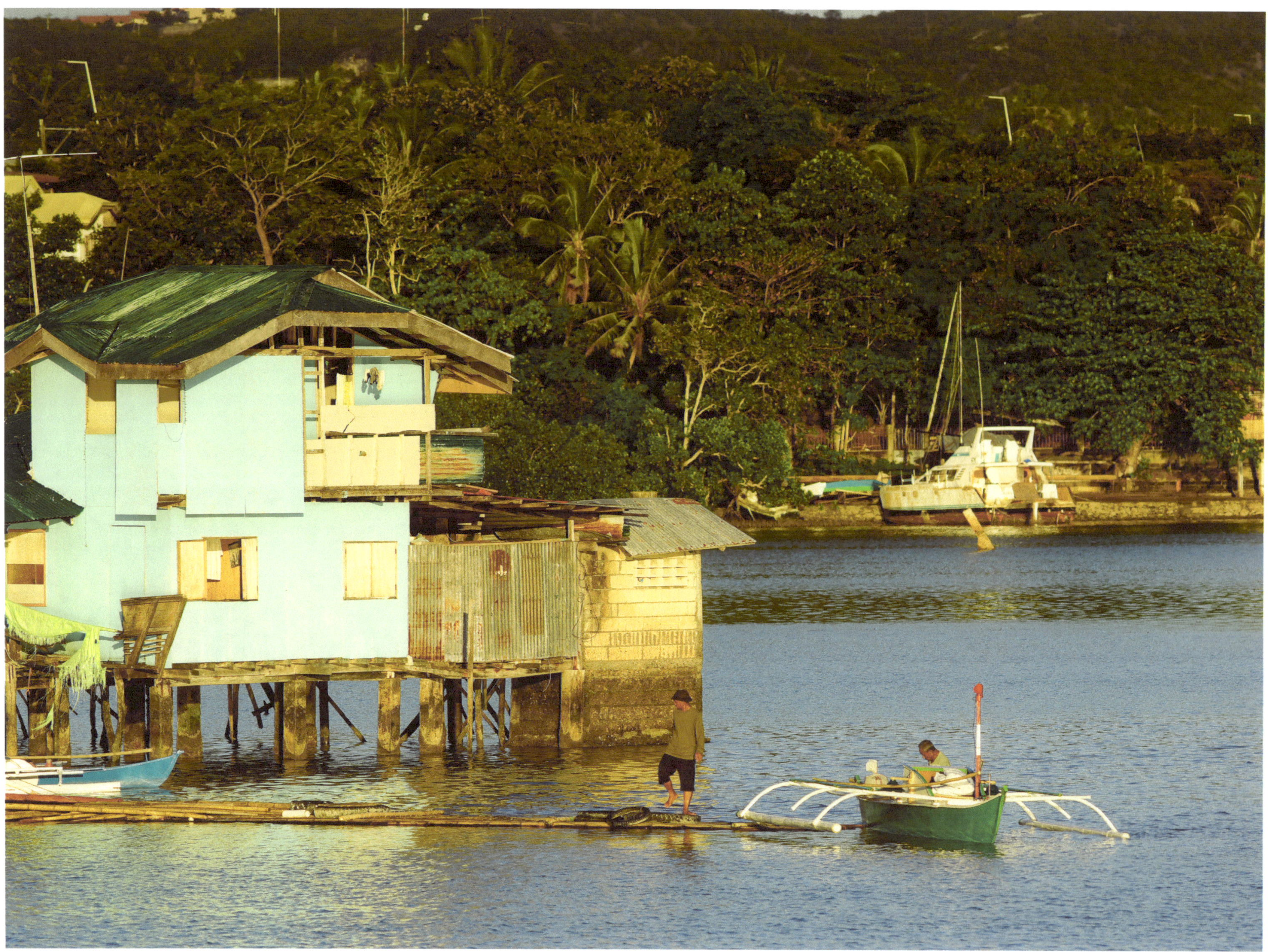

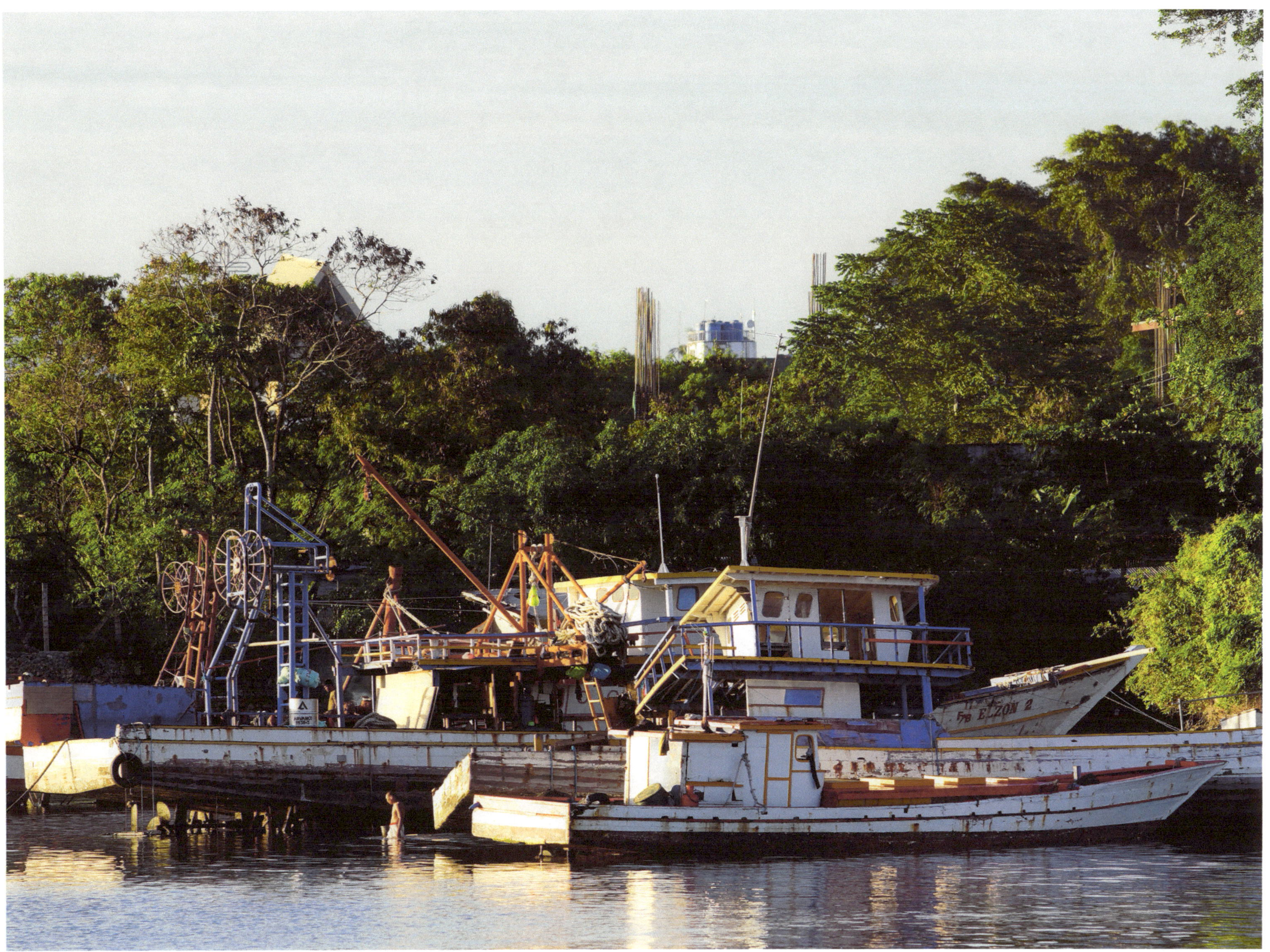
F/B ELZON 2

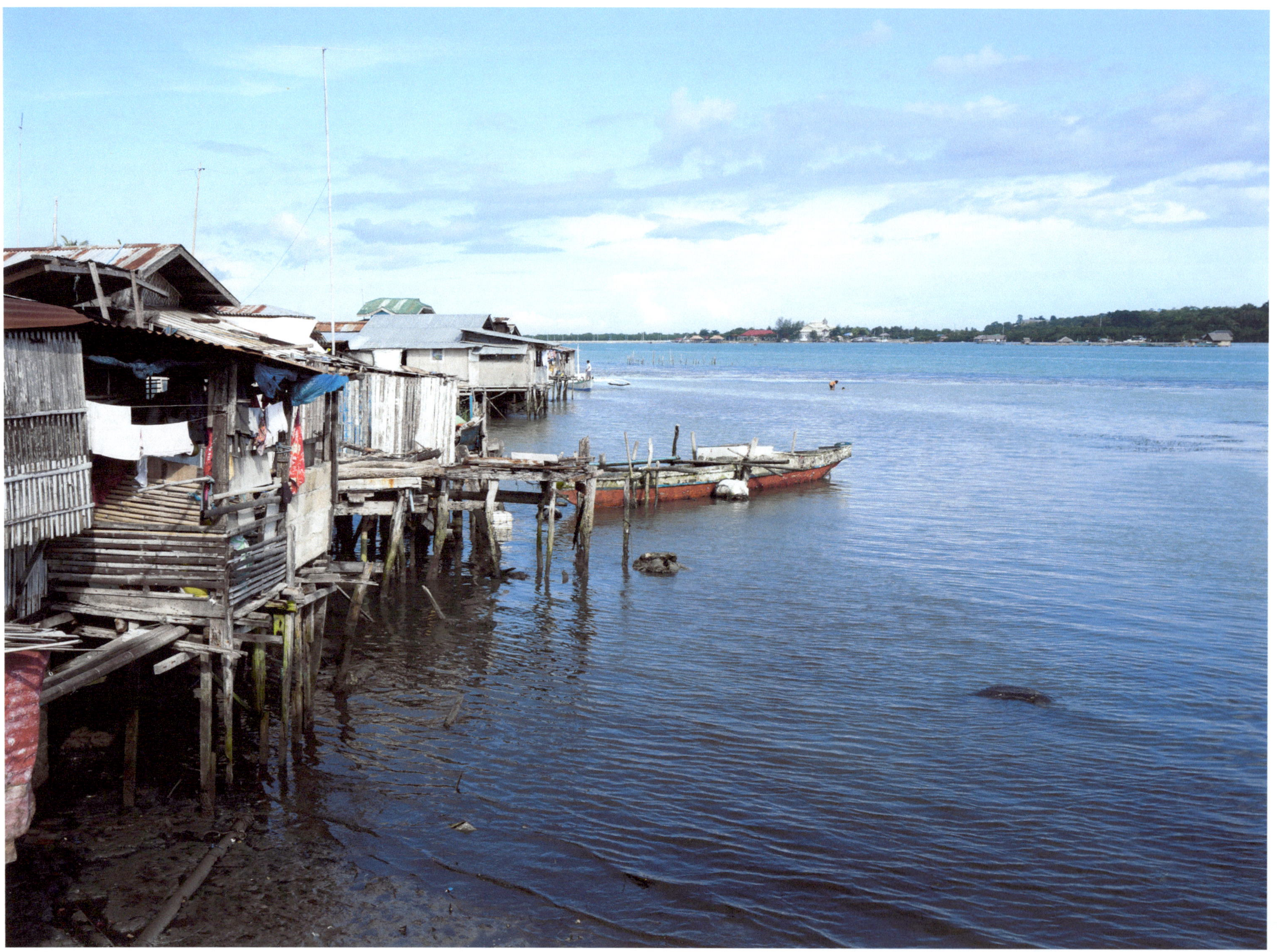

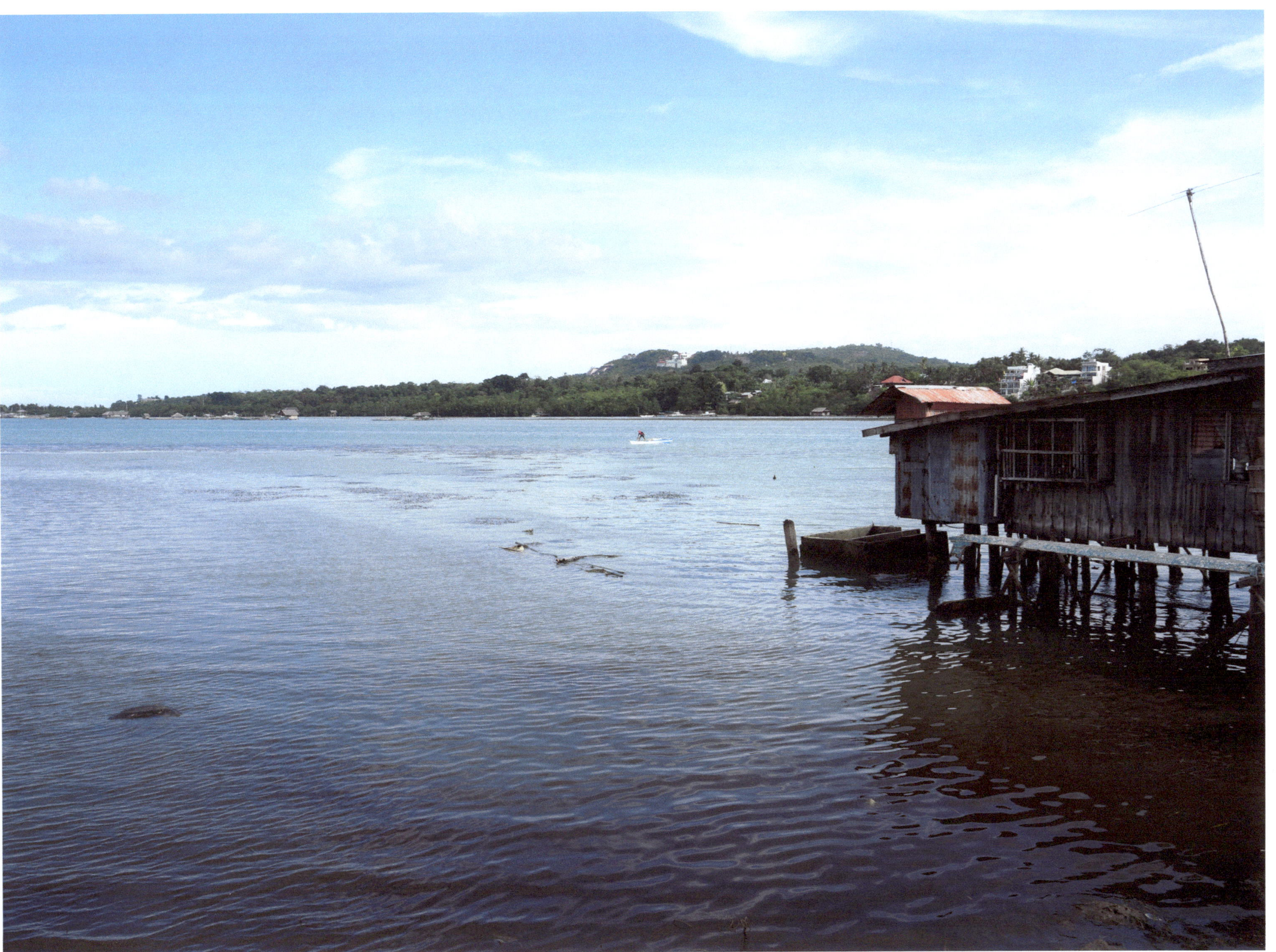

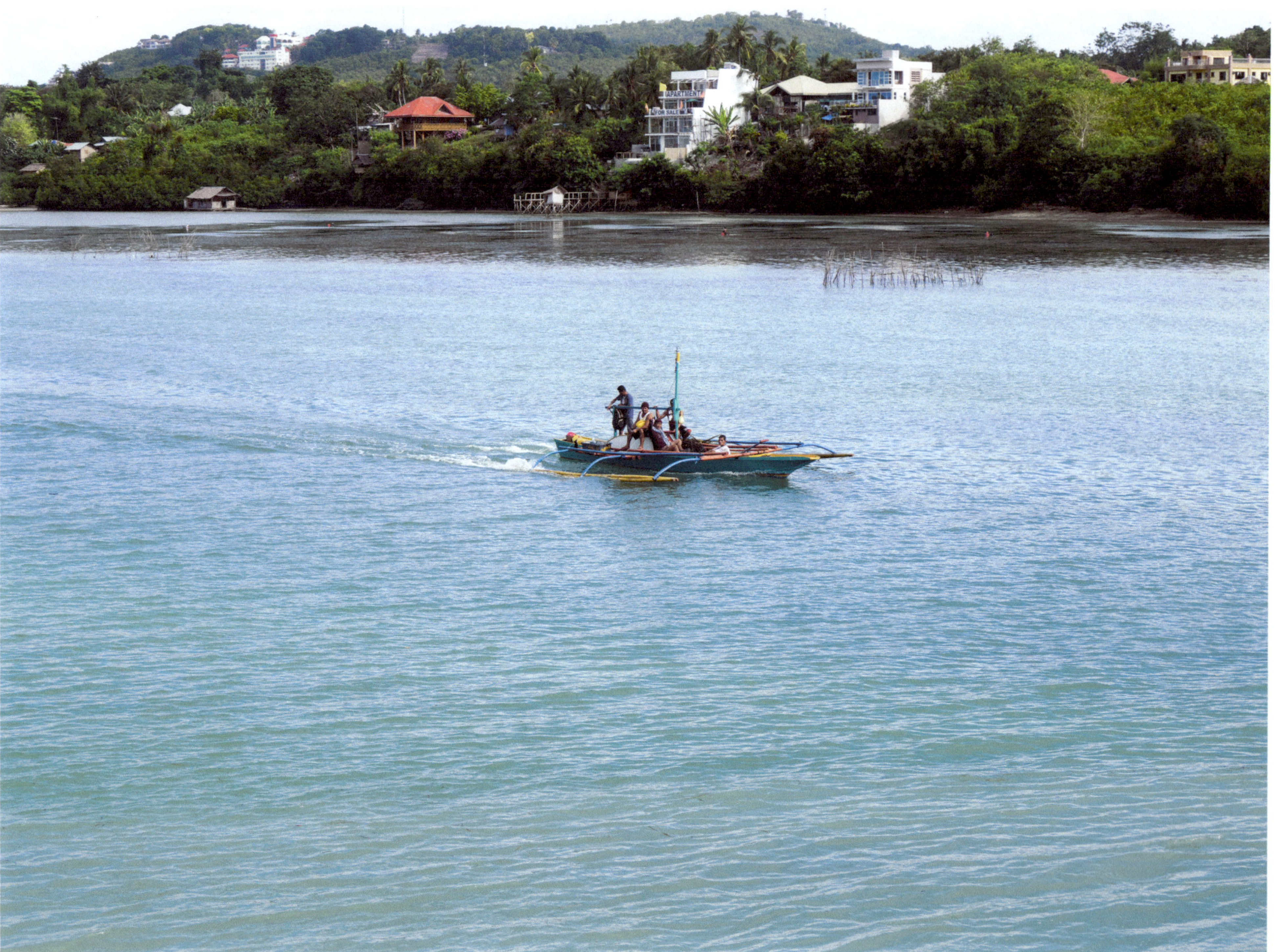
APARTMENT
FOR SALE

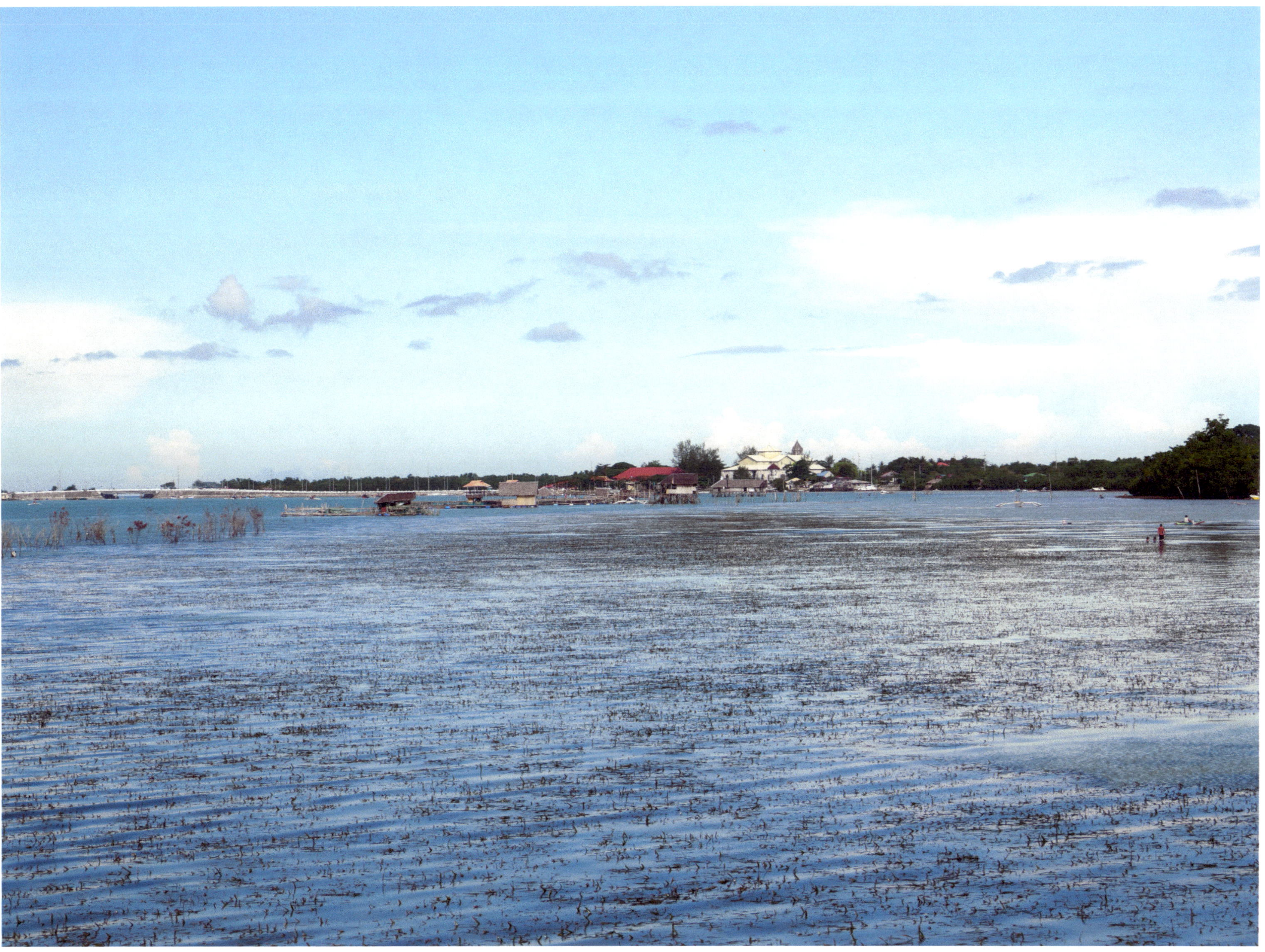

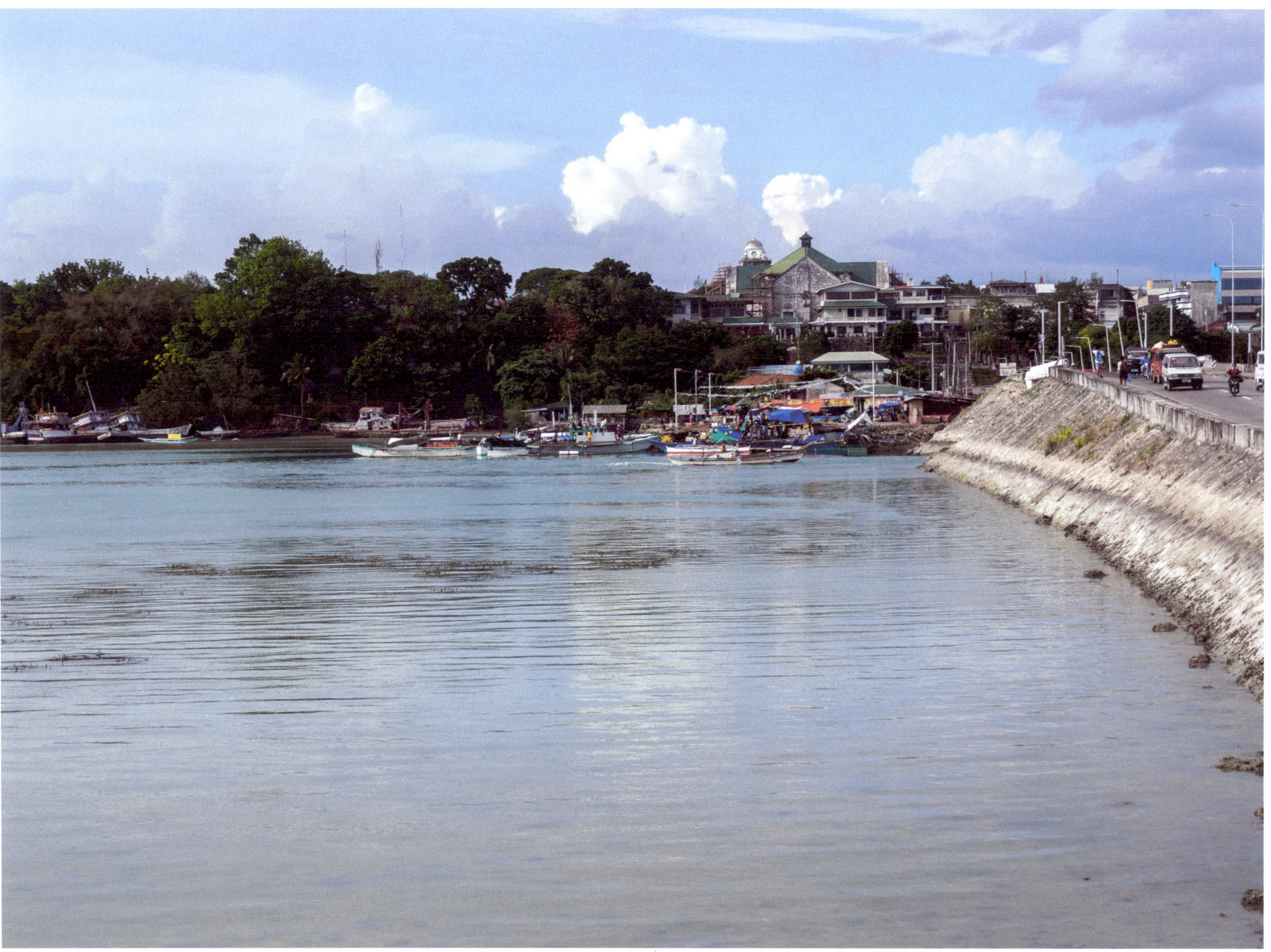

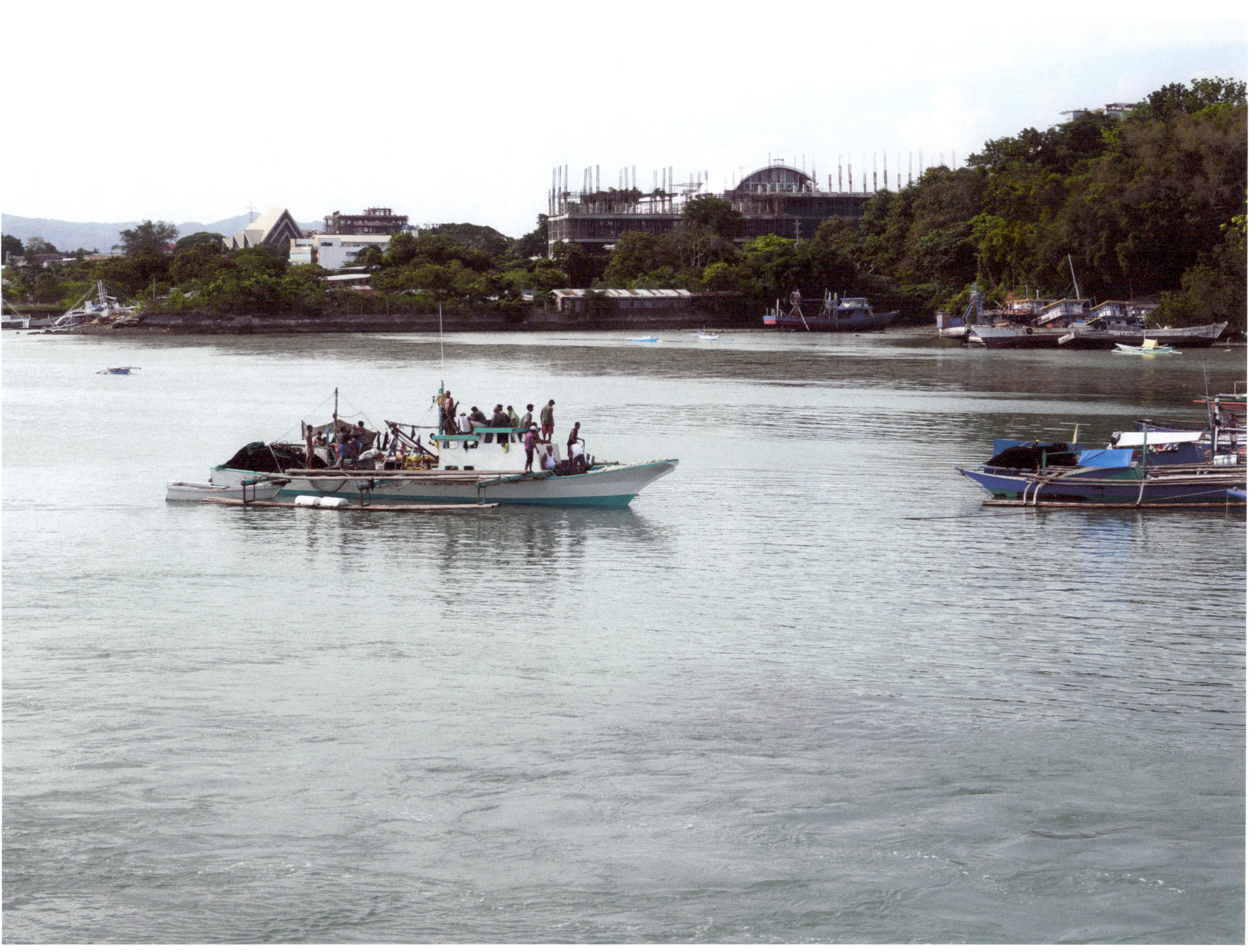

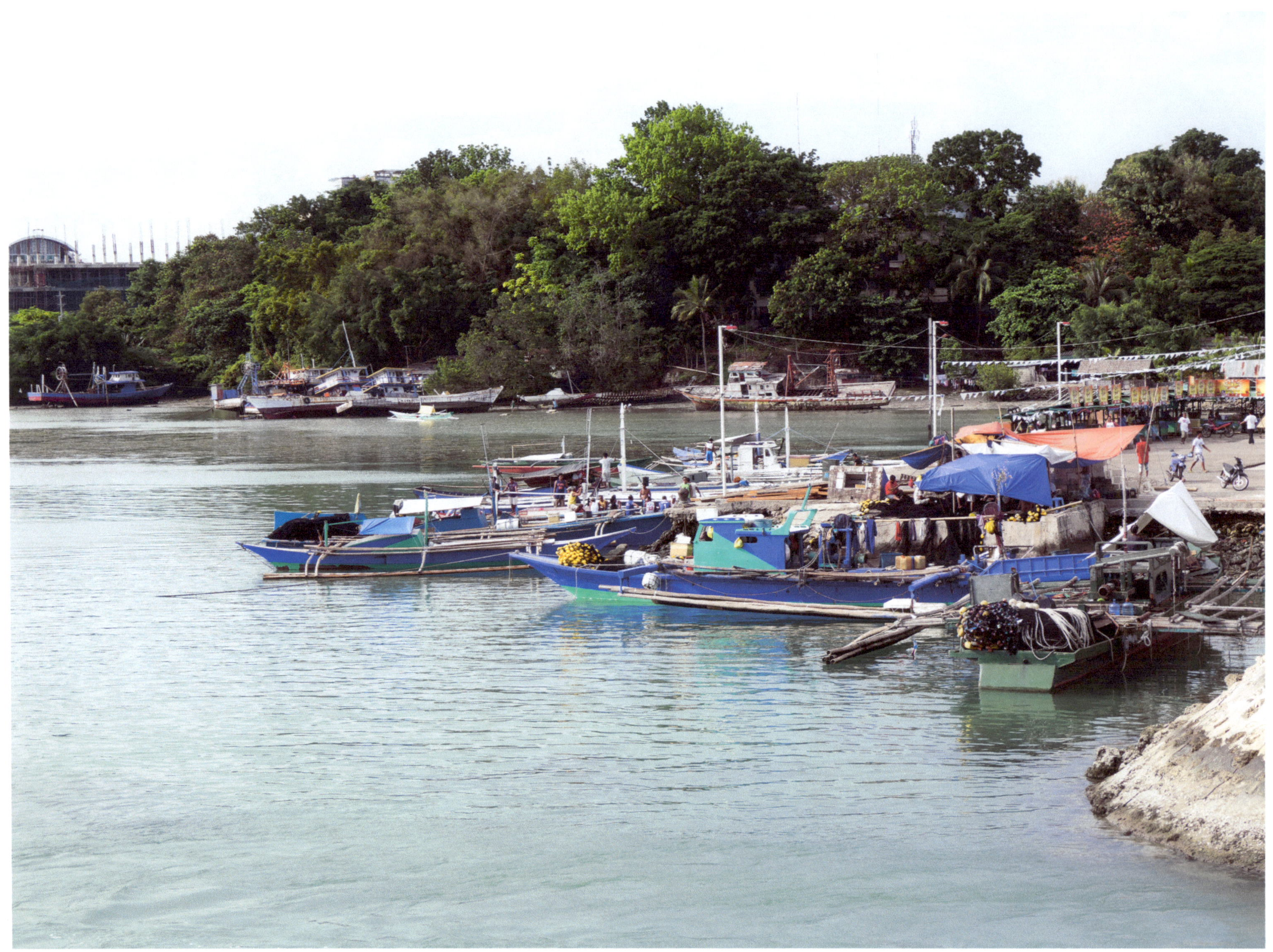

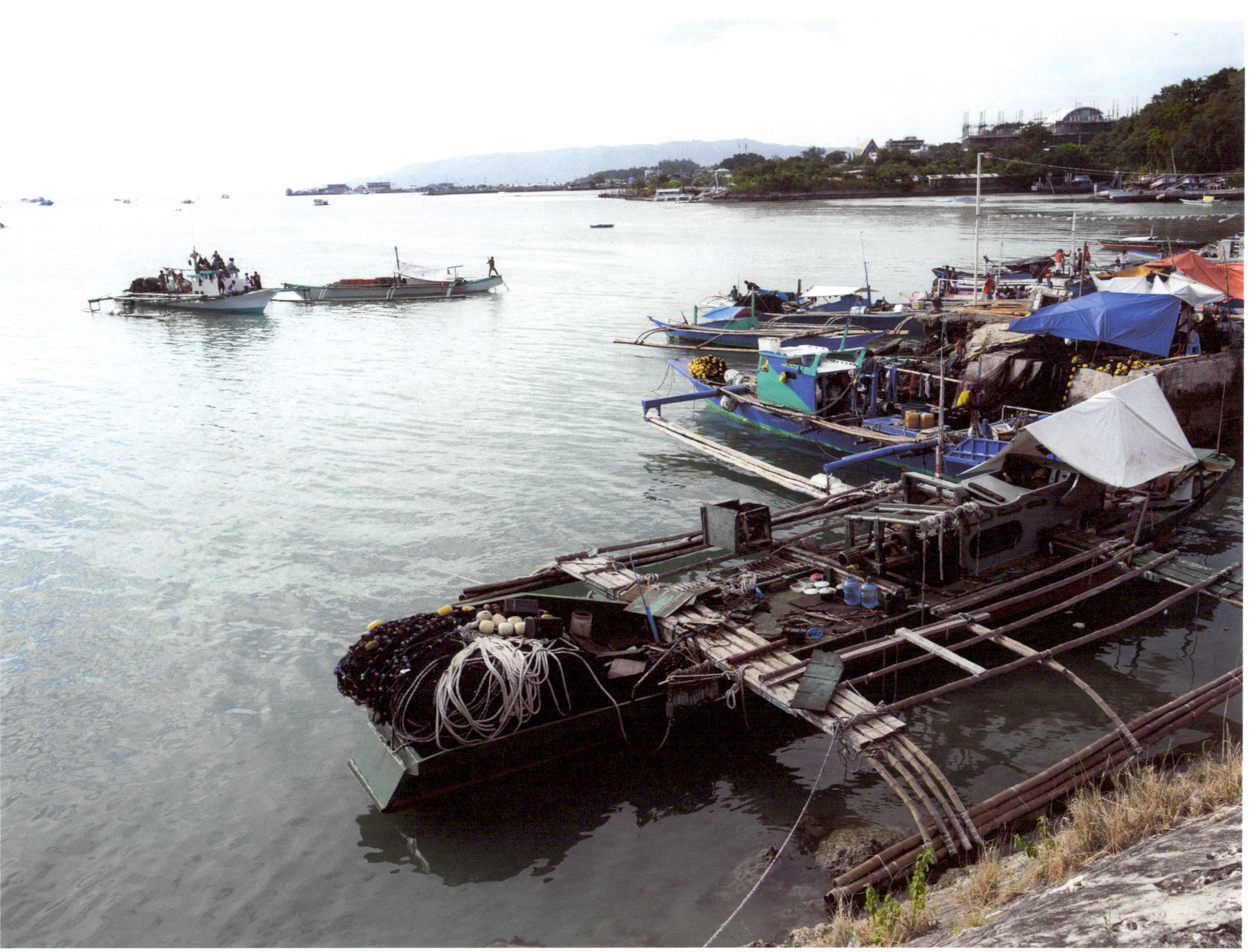

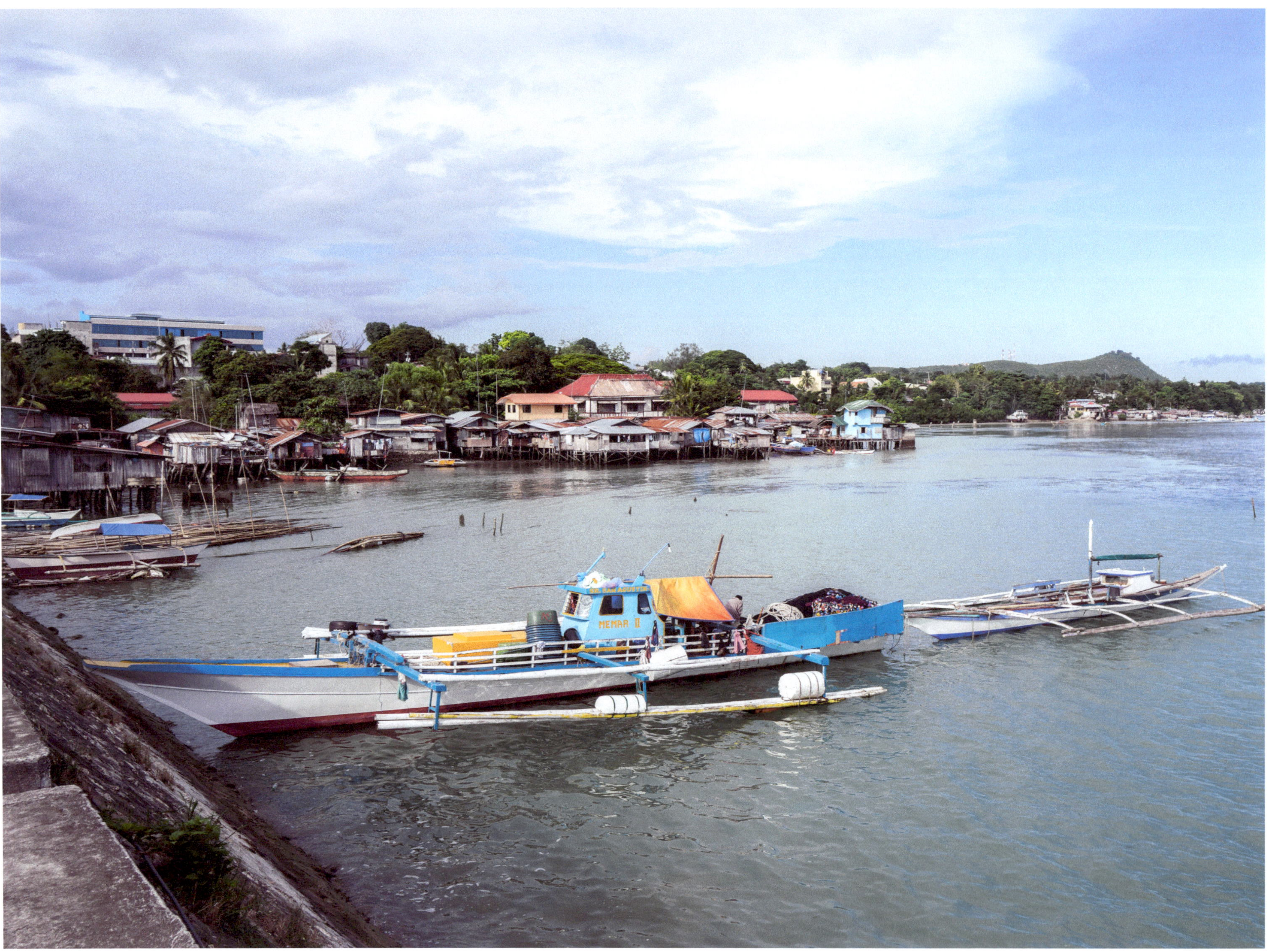
MEMAR II

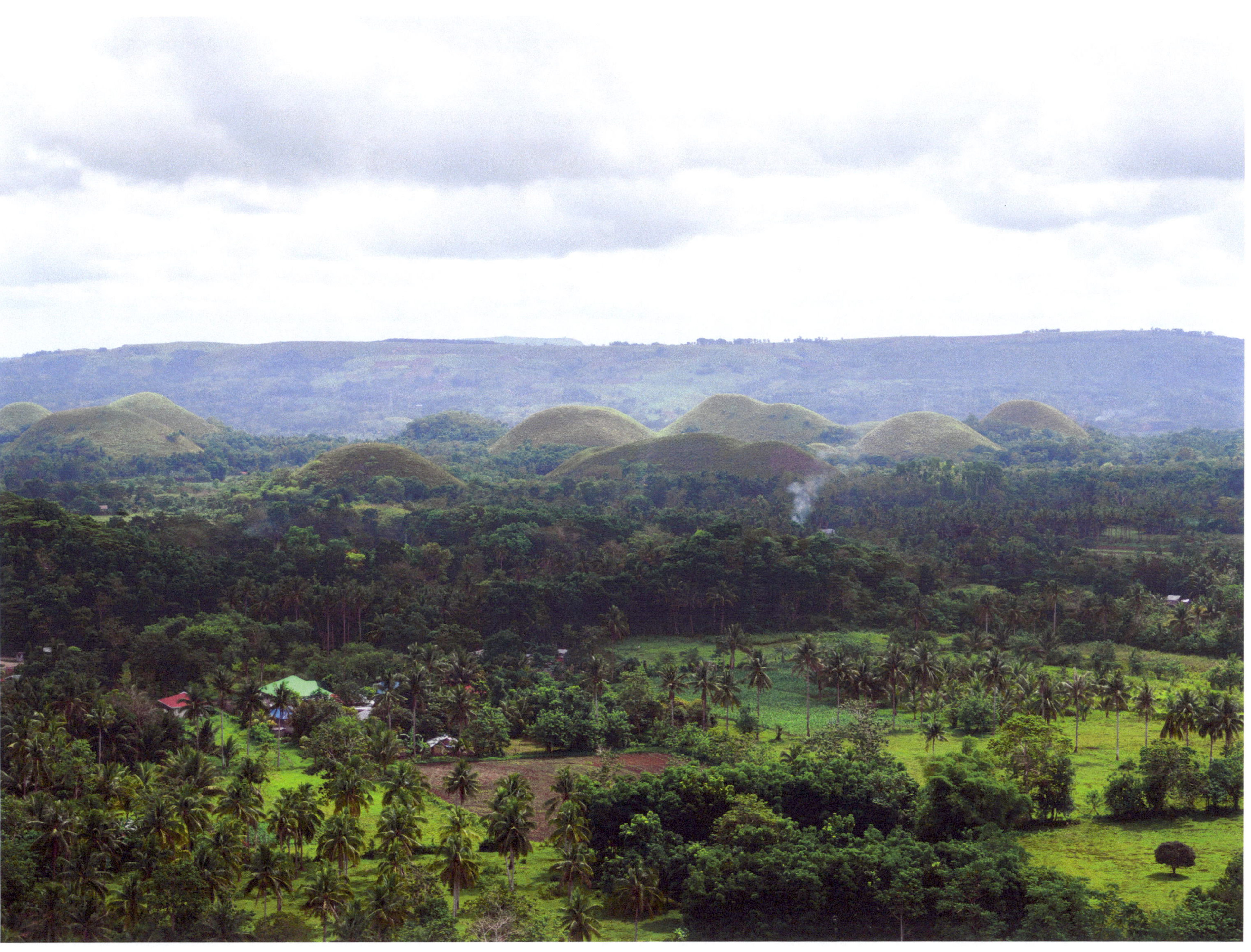

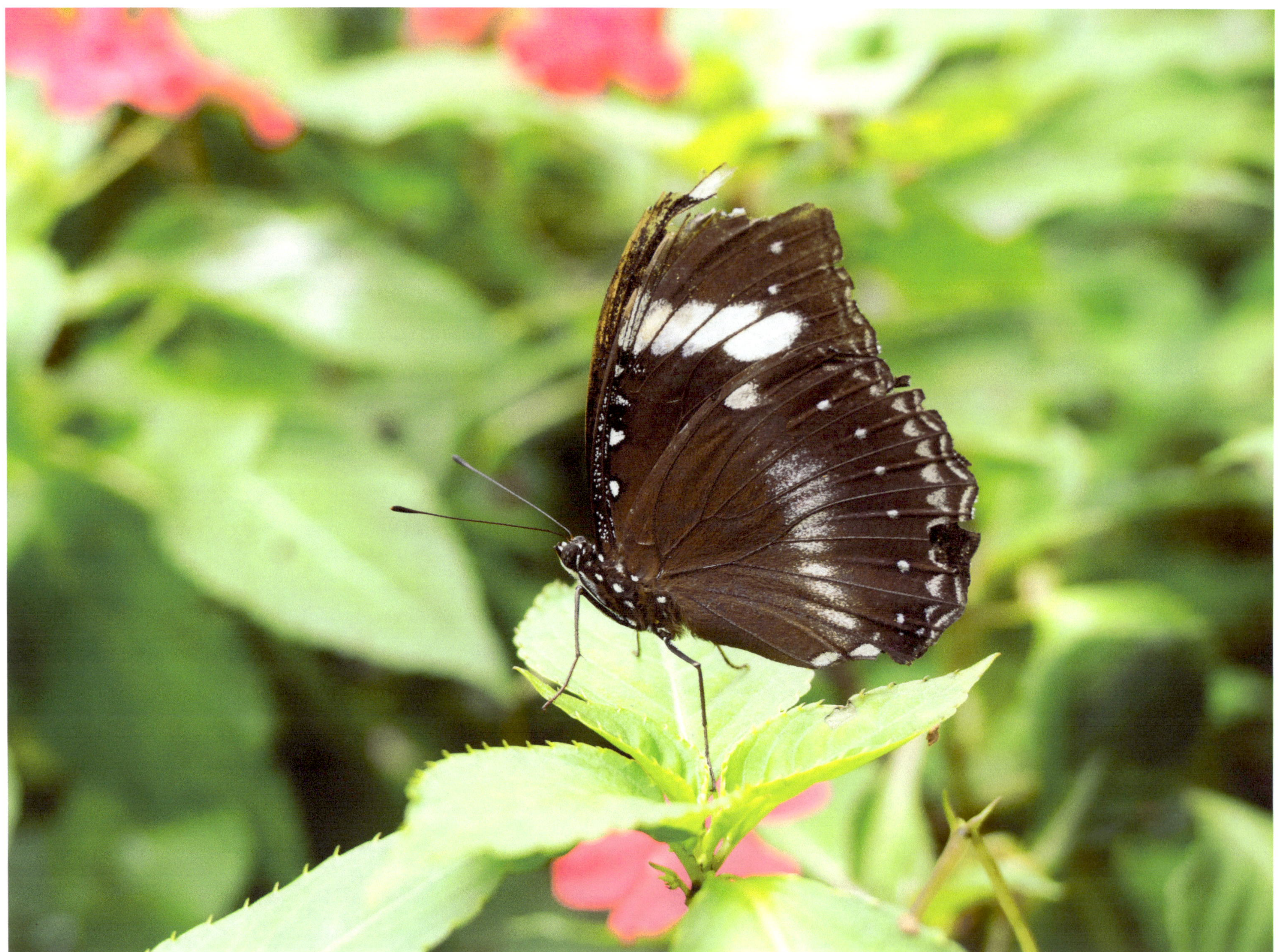

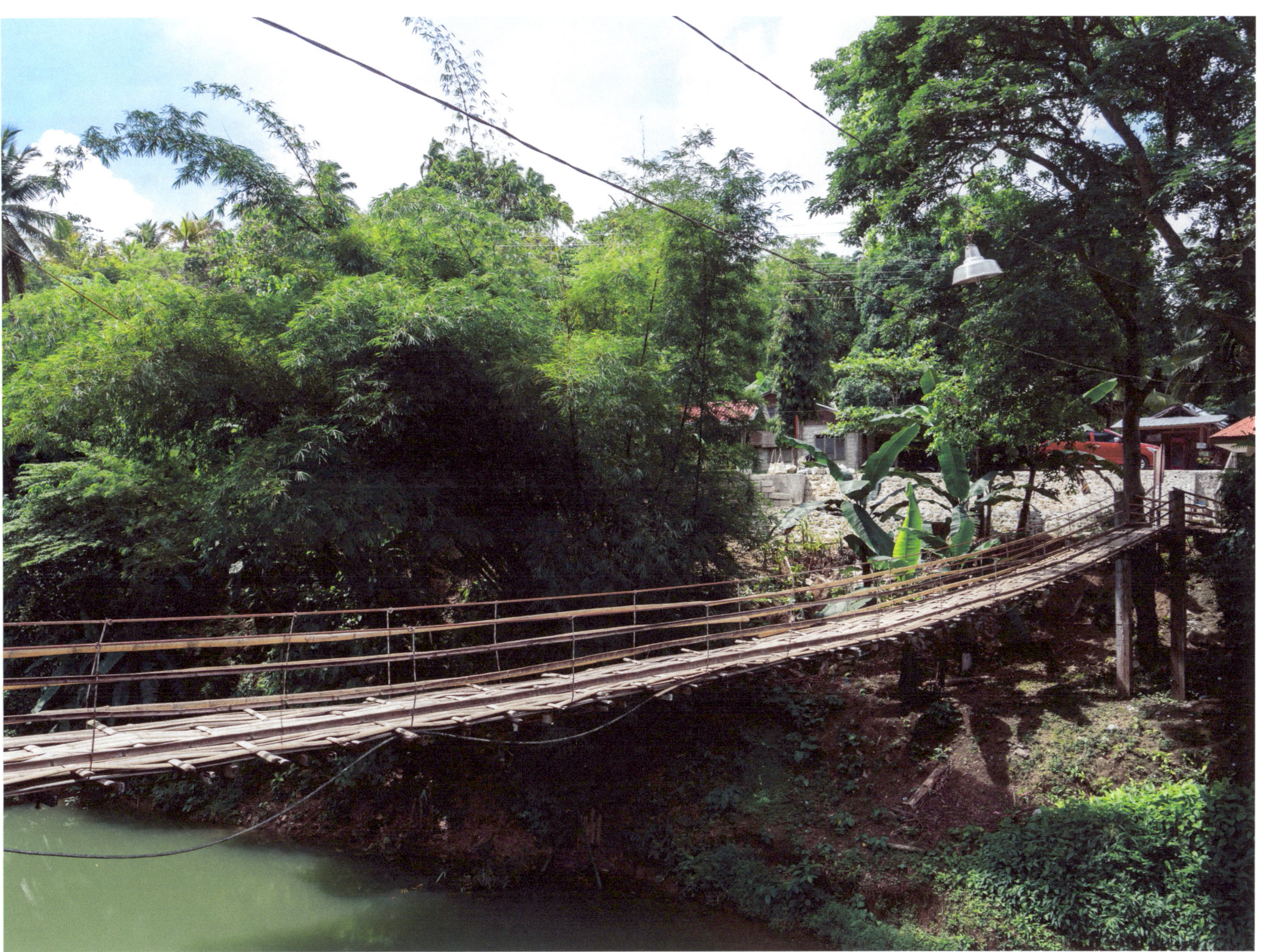

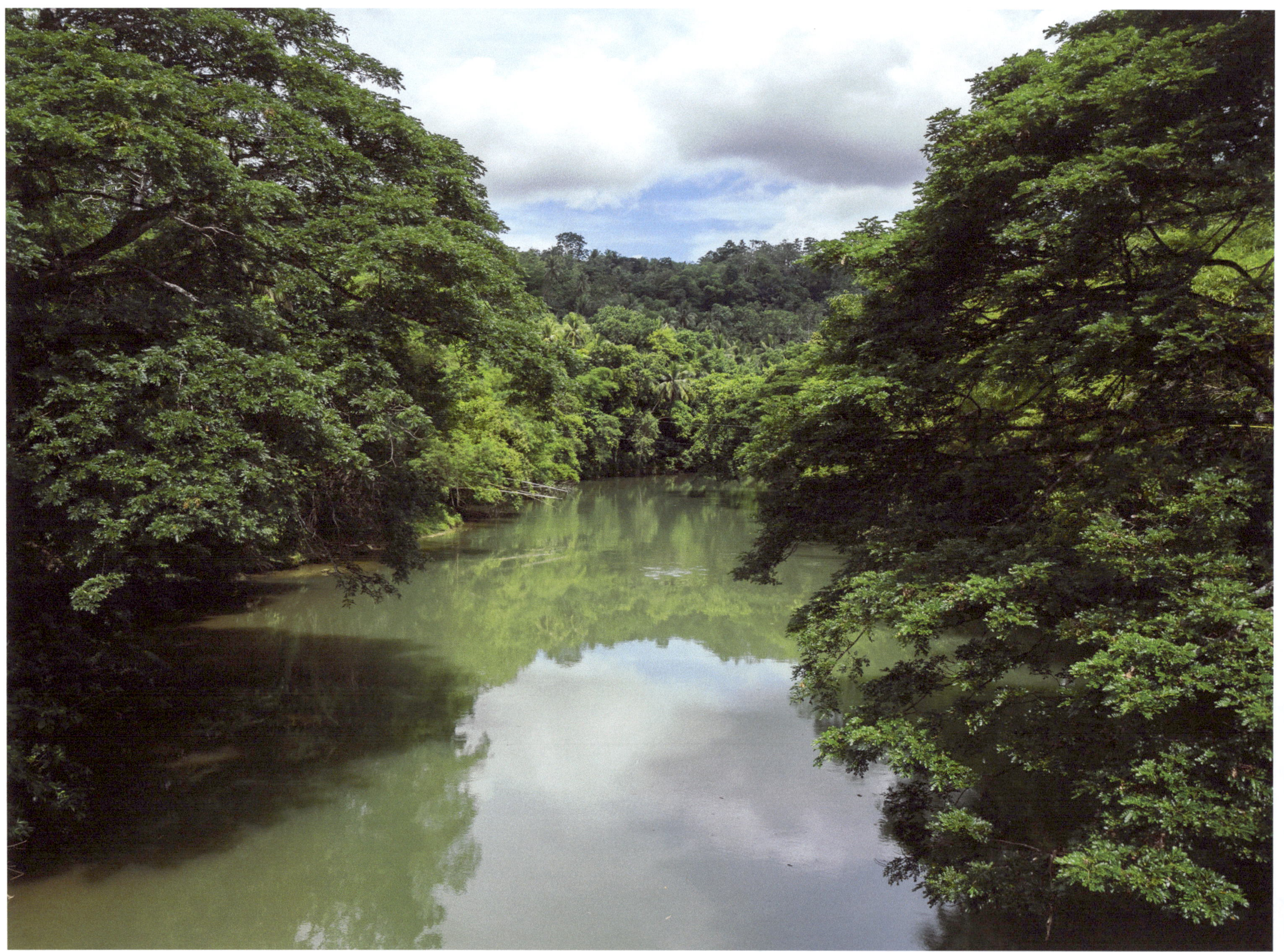

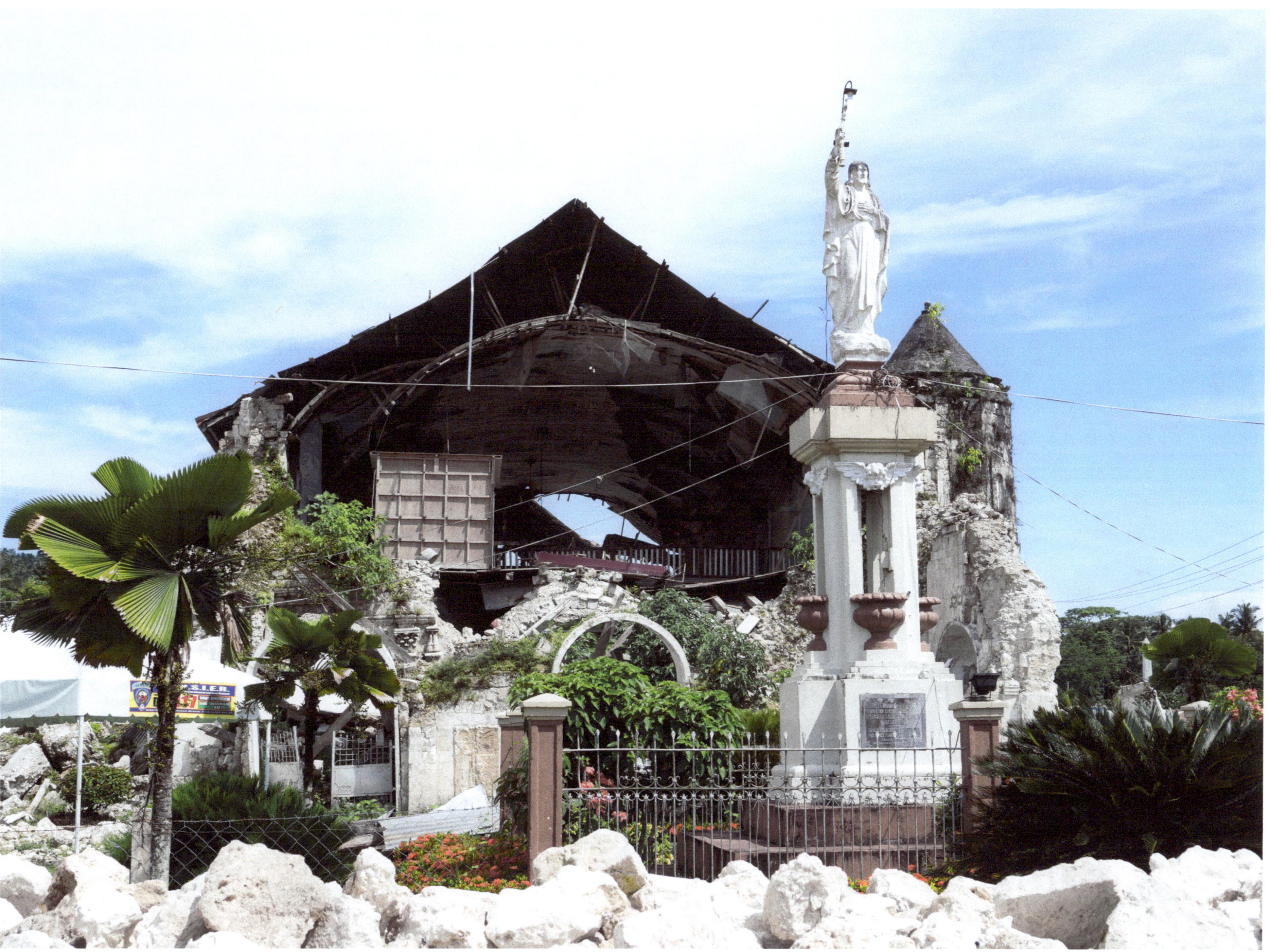

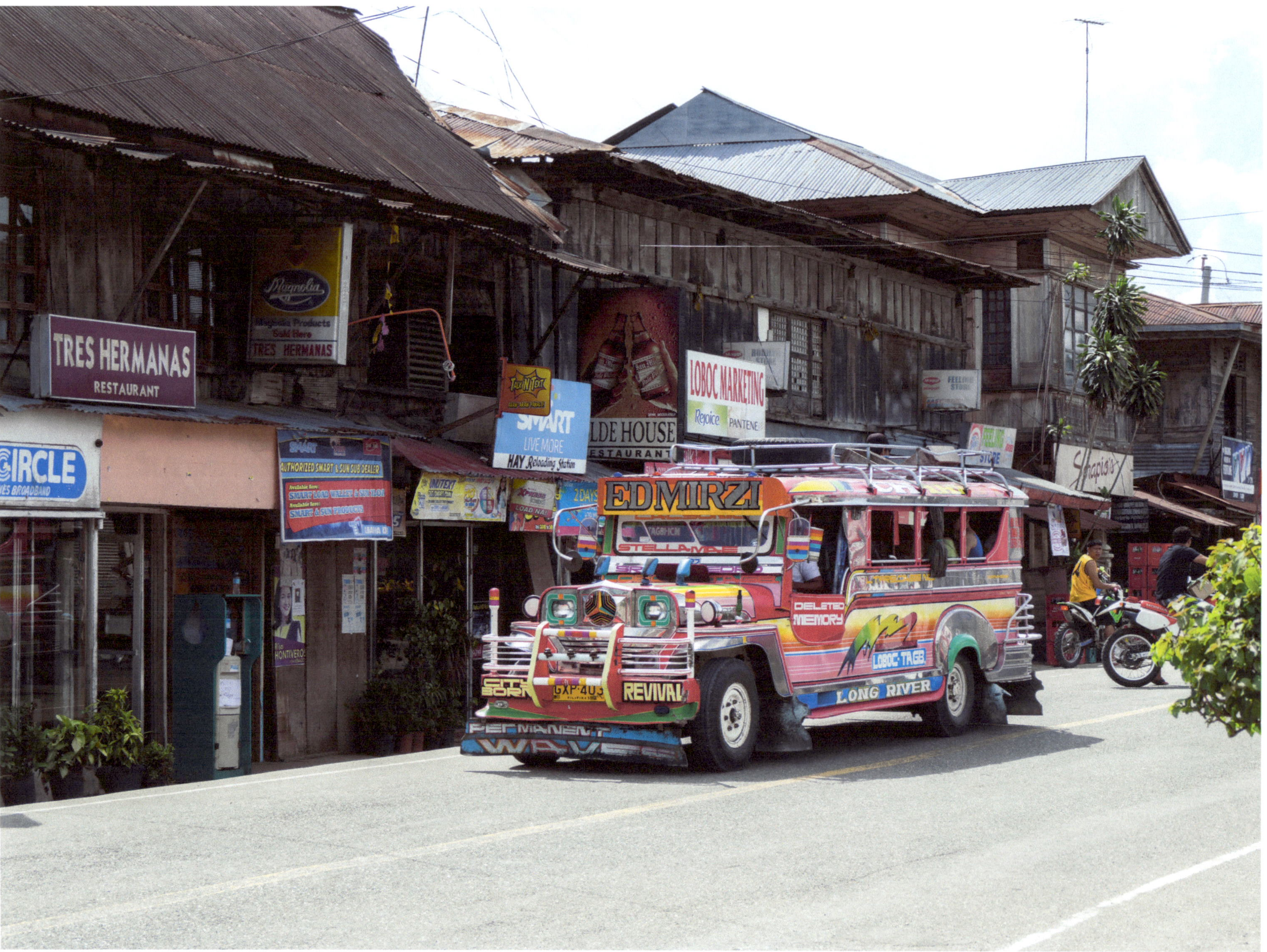

TRES HERMANAS
RESTAURANT
Magnolia
Magnolia Products
Sold Here
TRES HERMANAS
SMART
LIVE MORE
HAY Reloading Station
LOBOC MARKETING
Rejoice
PANTENE
AUTHORIZED SMART & SUN SUB DEALER
2 DAYS
EDMIRZI
STELLA MAE
DELETED
MEMORY
LOBOC-TAGB.
LONG RIVER
REVIVAL
PERMANENT

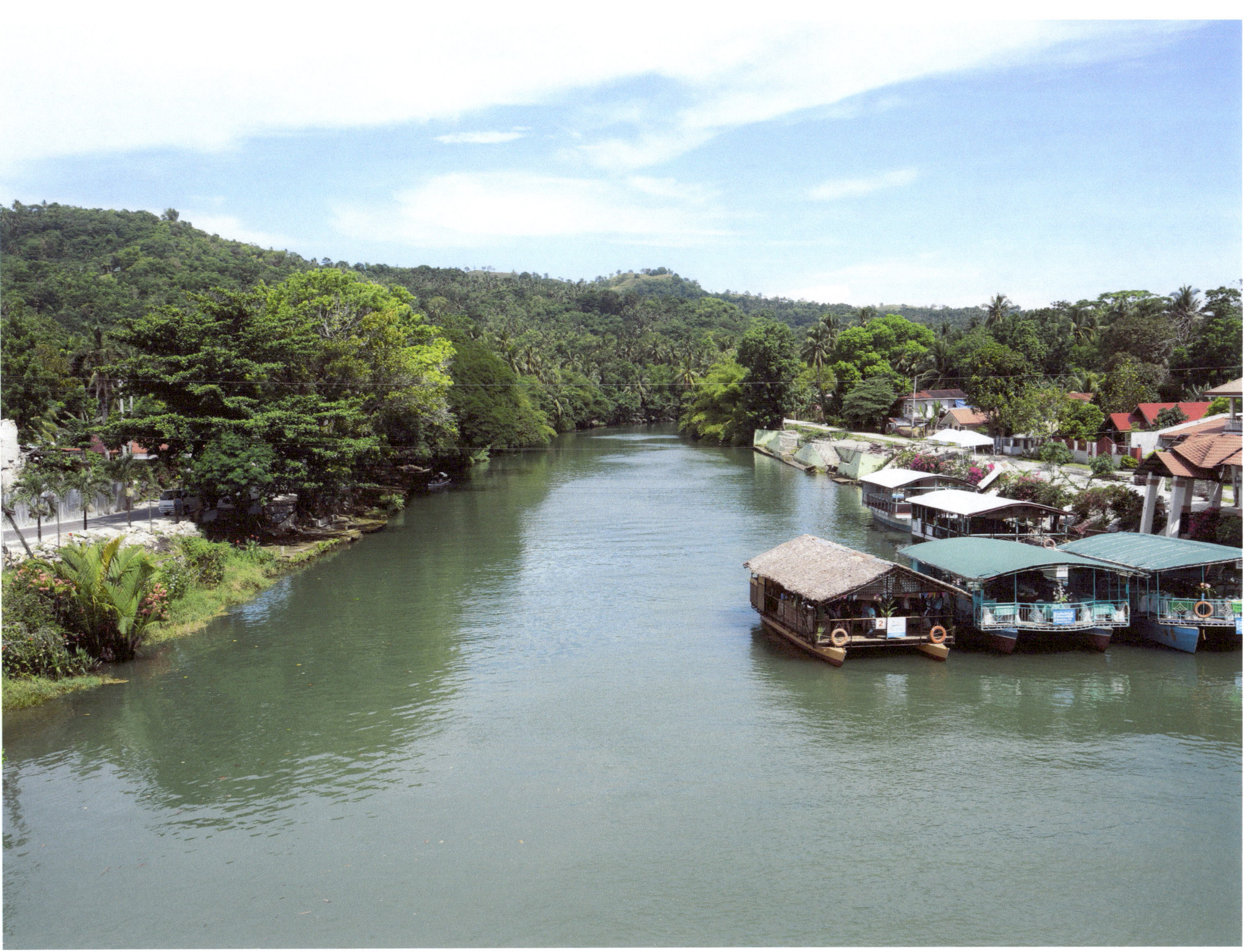

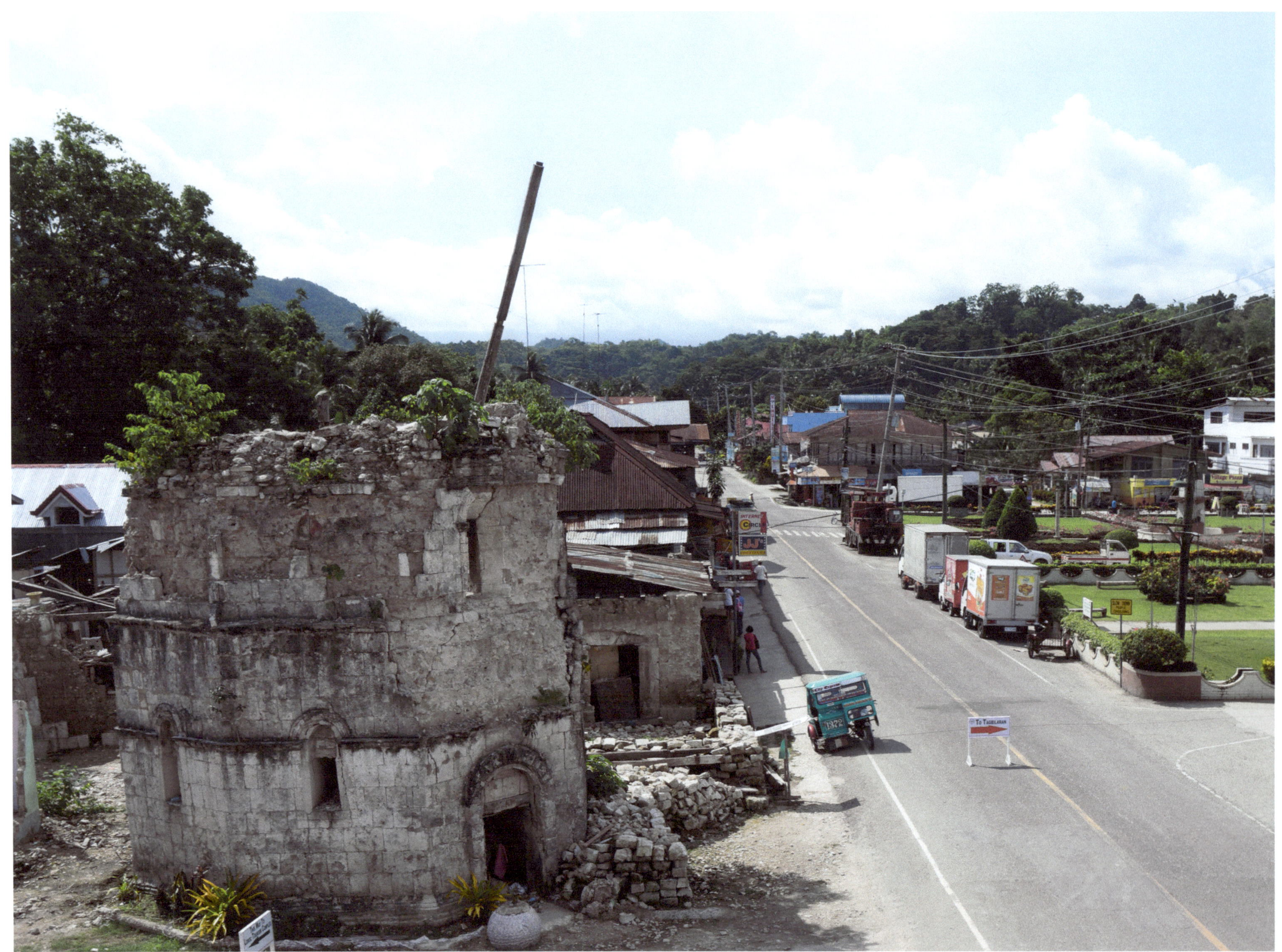
To Tagbilaran

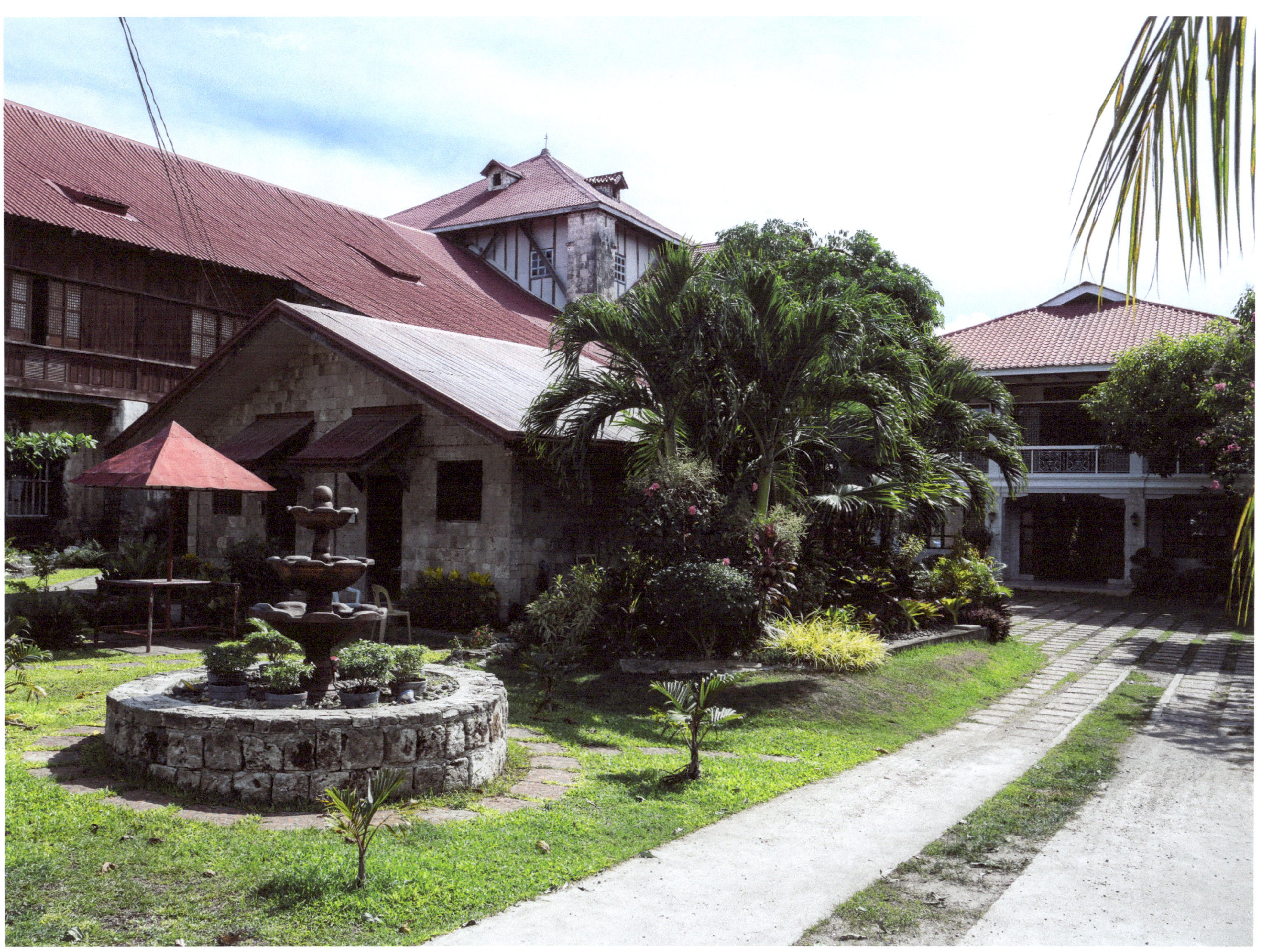

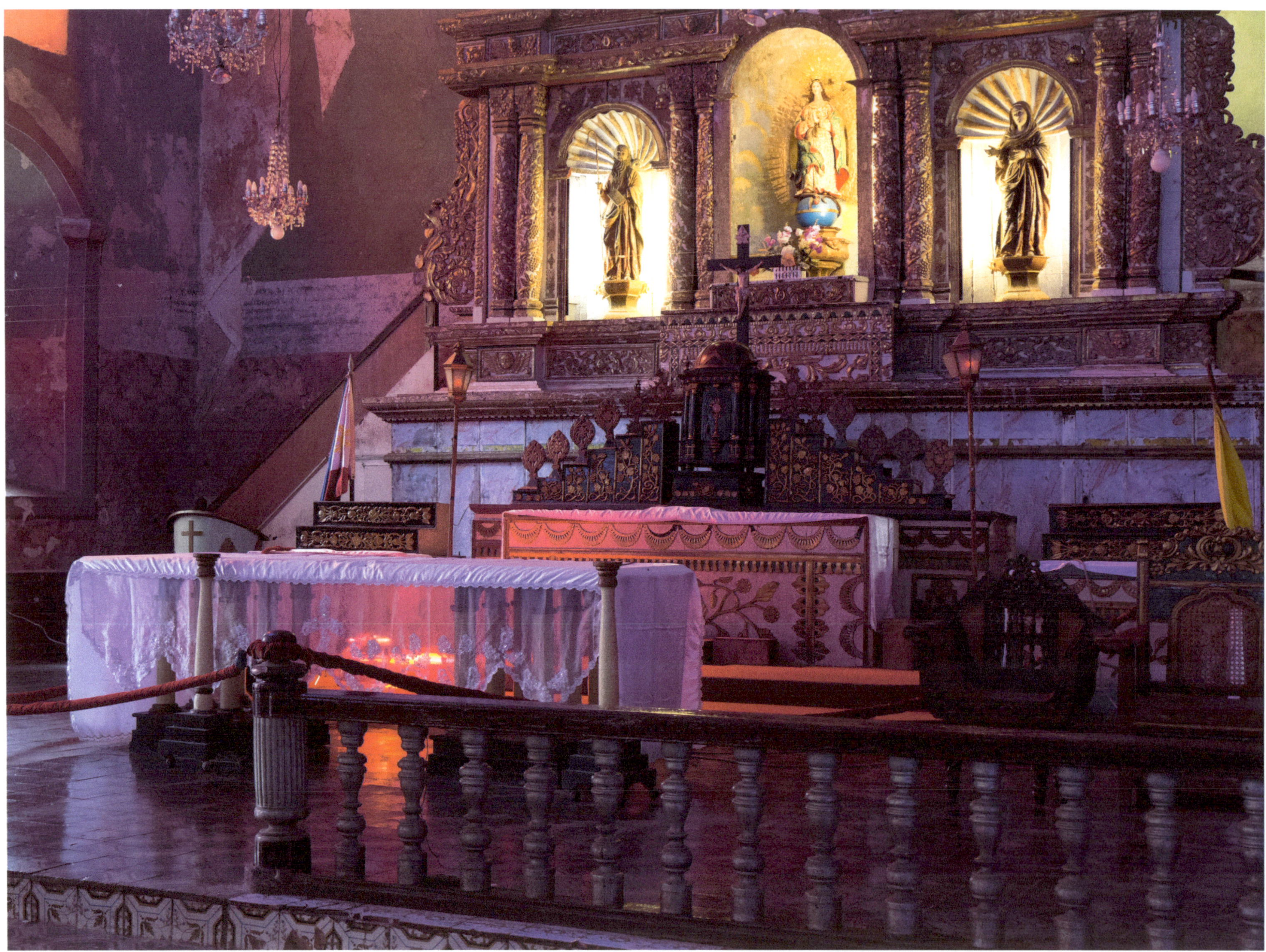

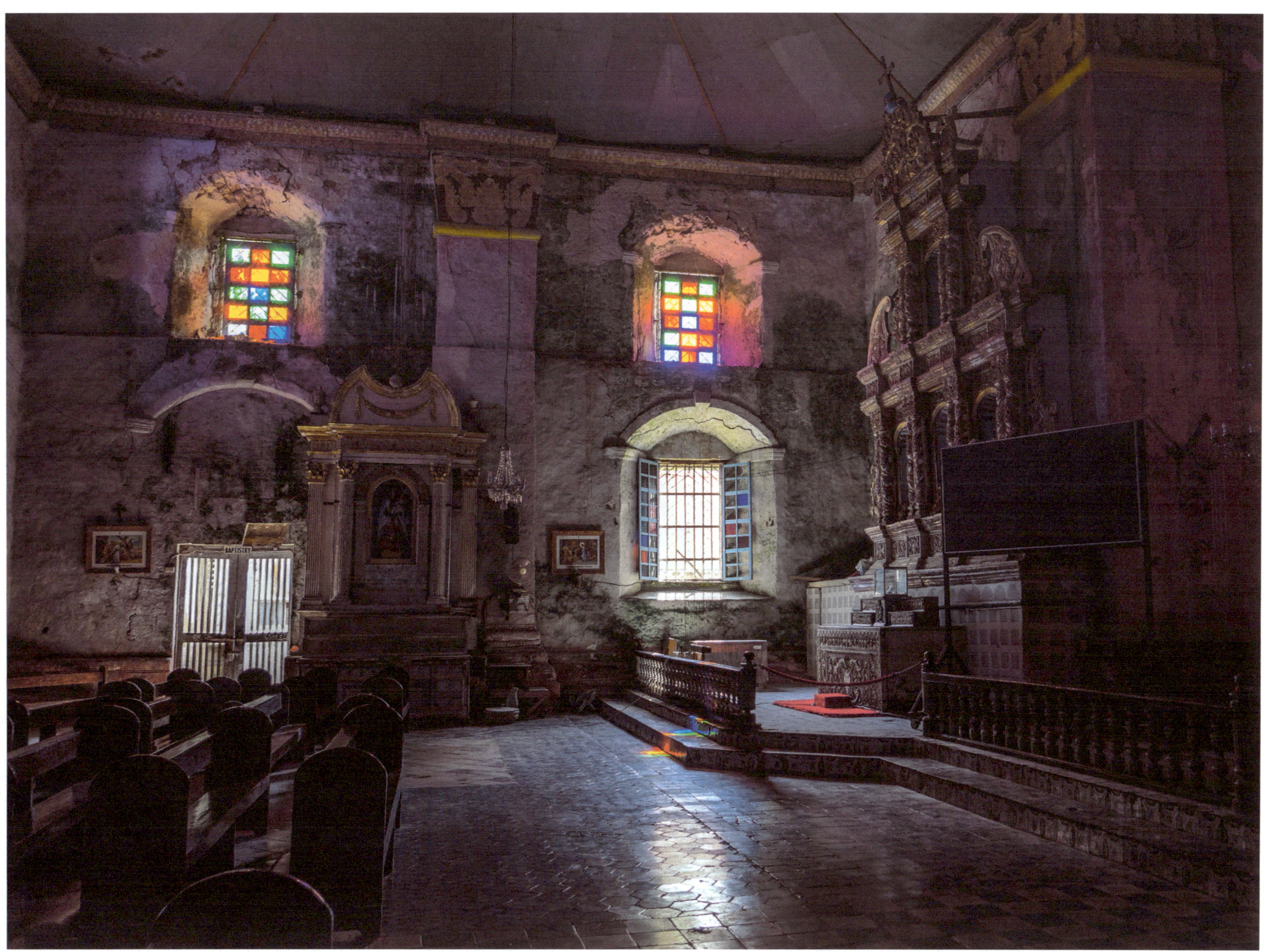
BAPTISTRY

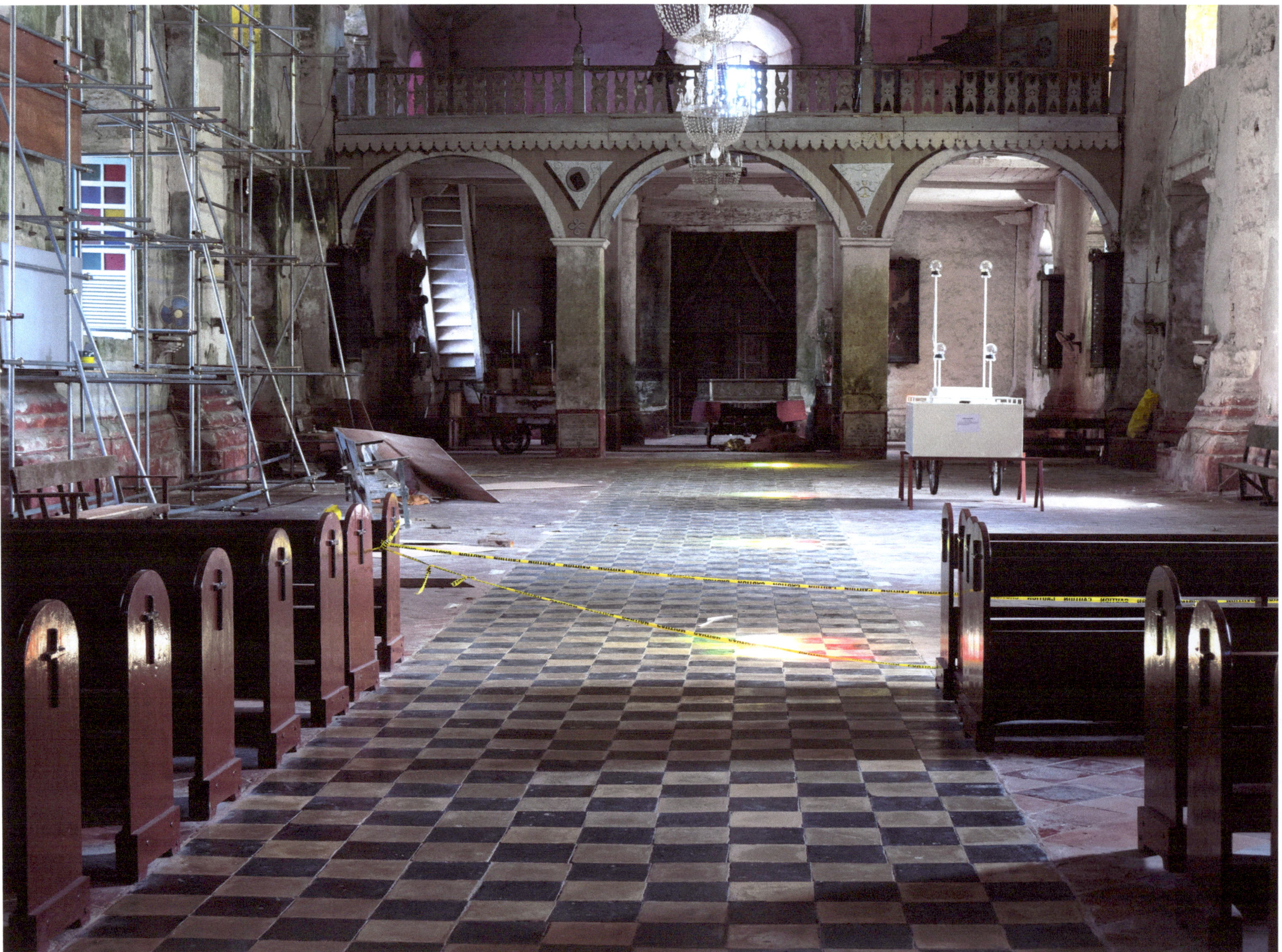

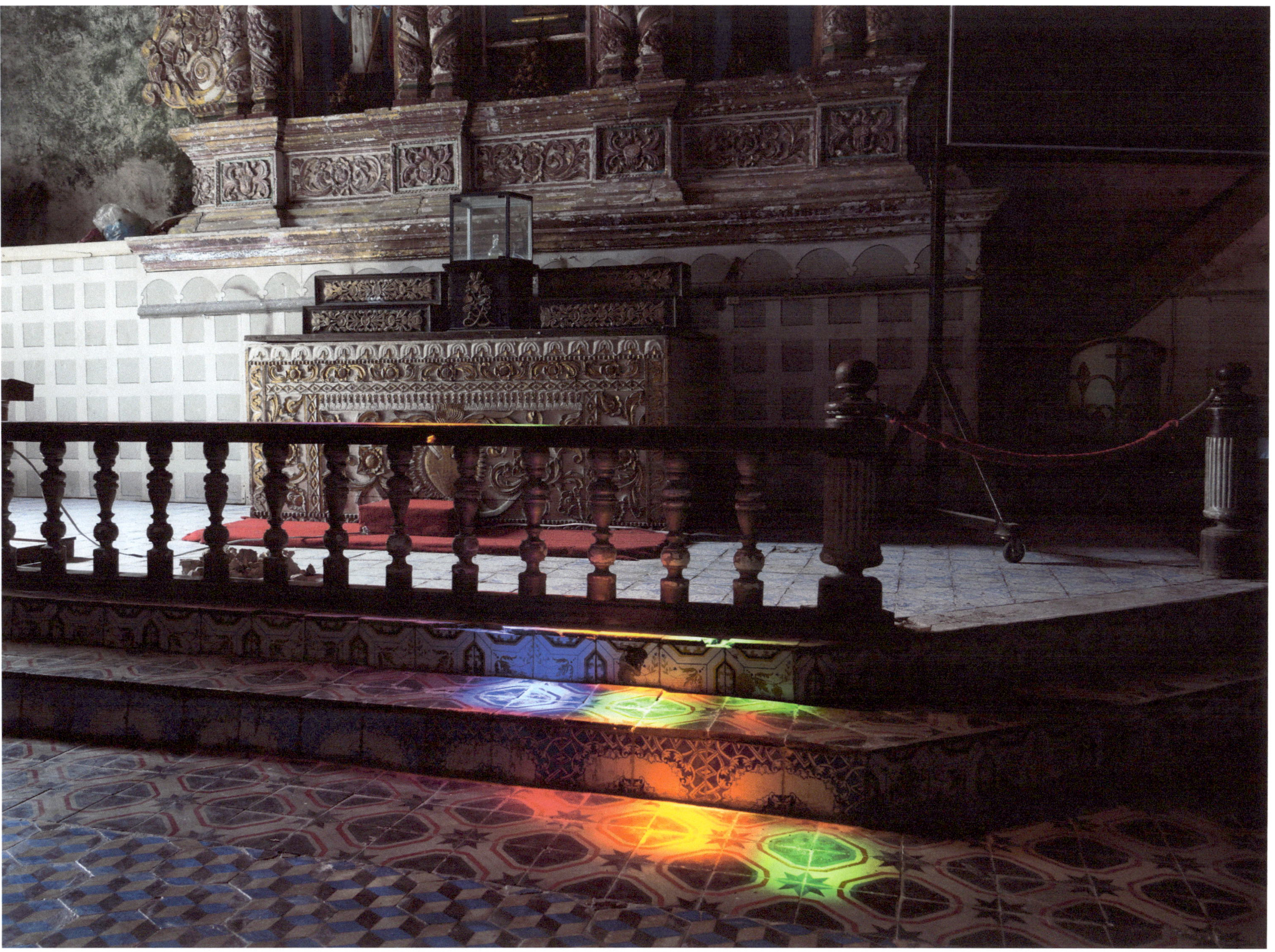

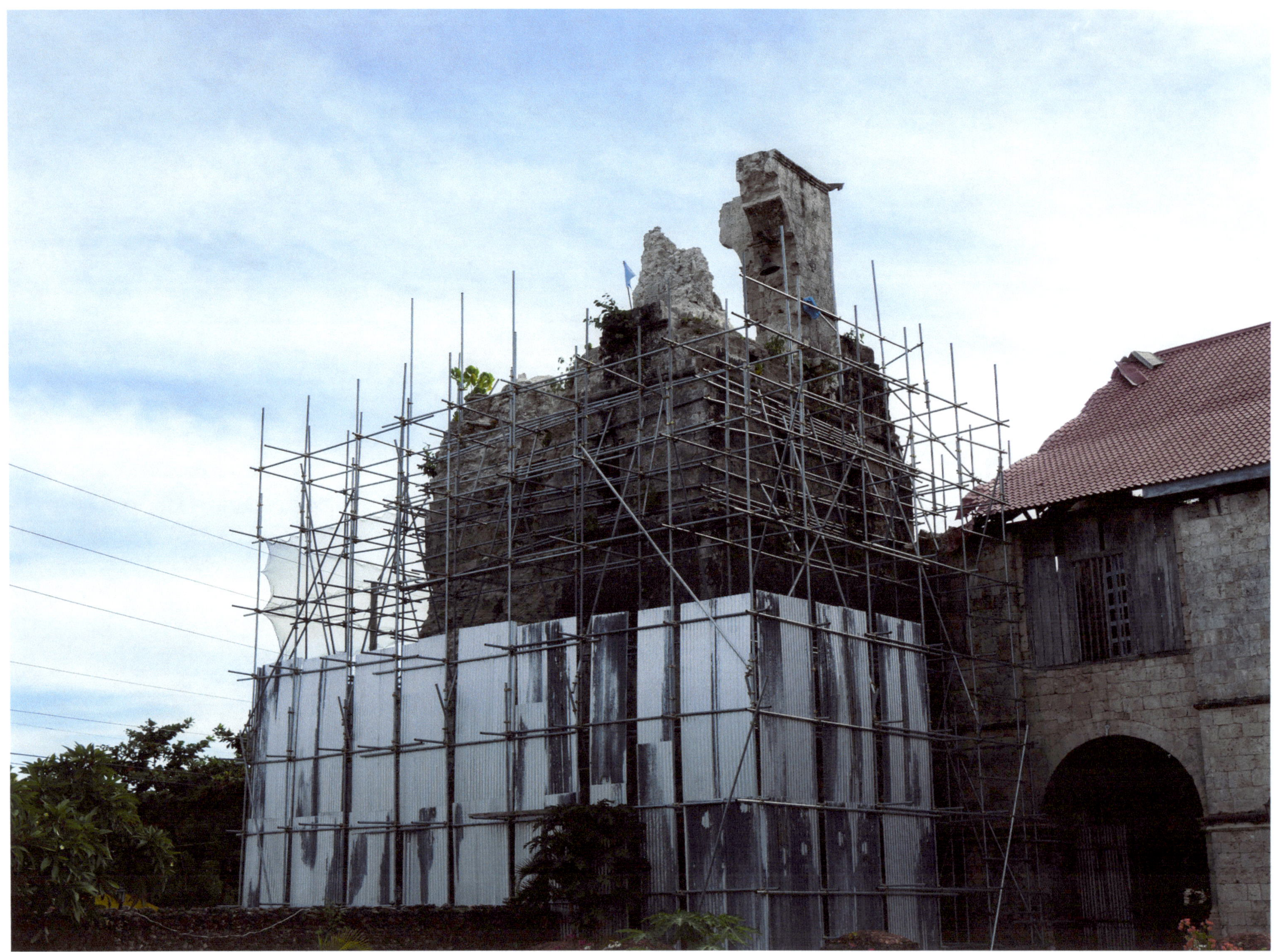

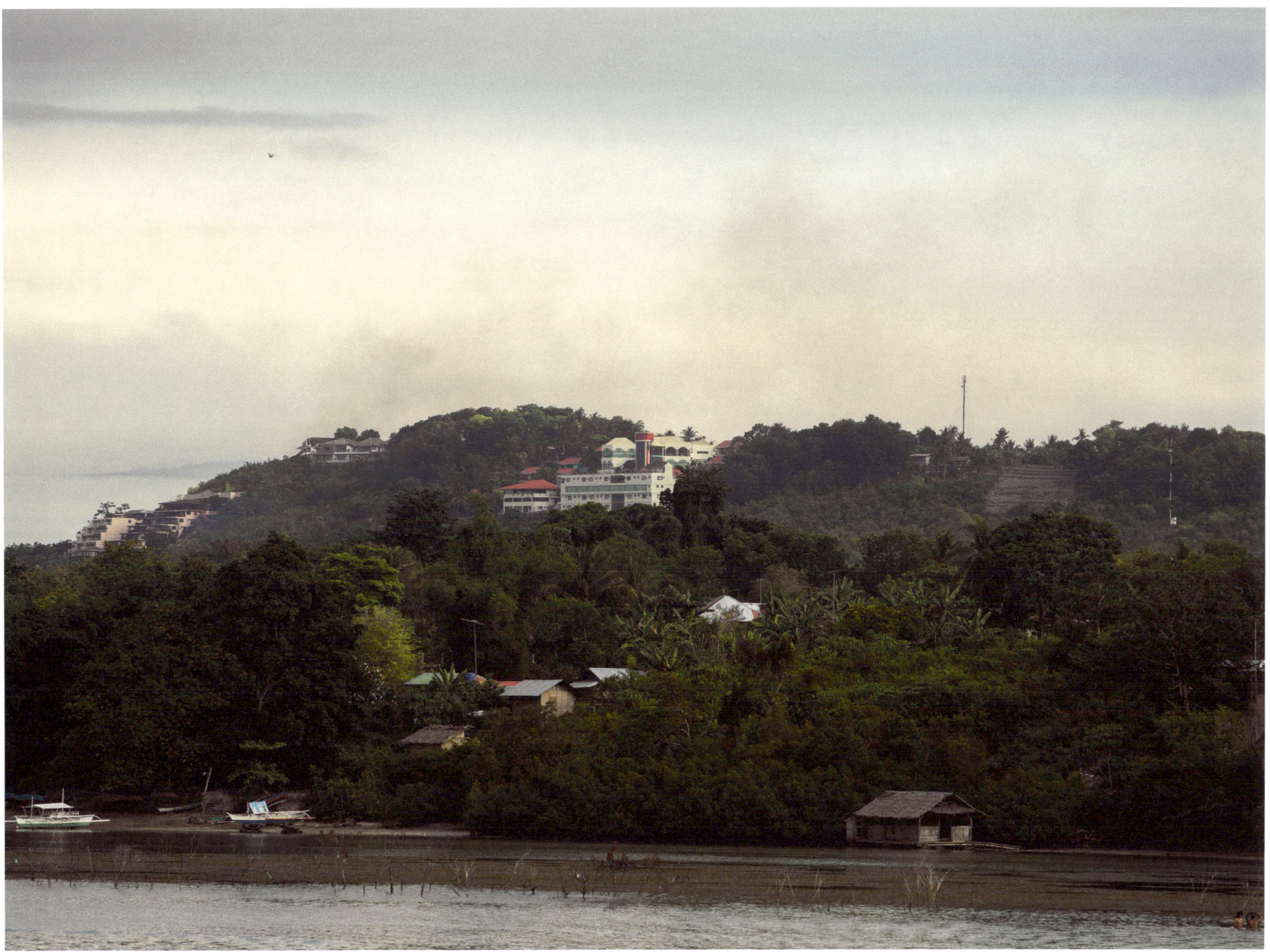

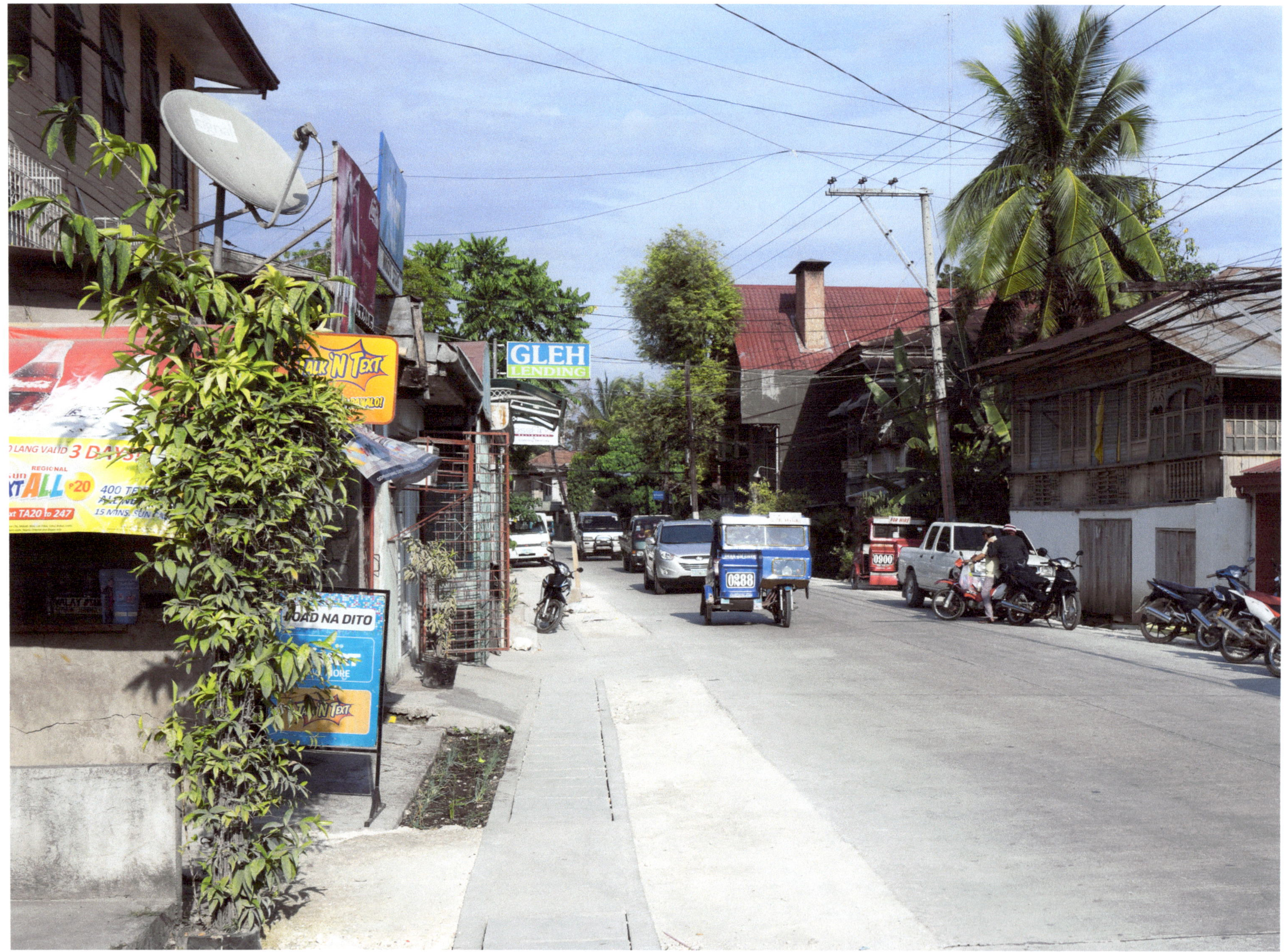
GLEH
LENDING

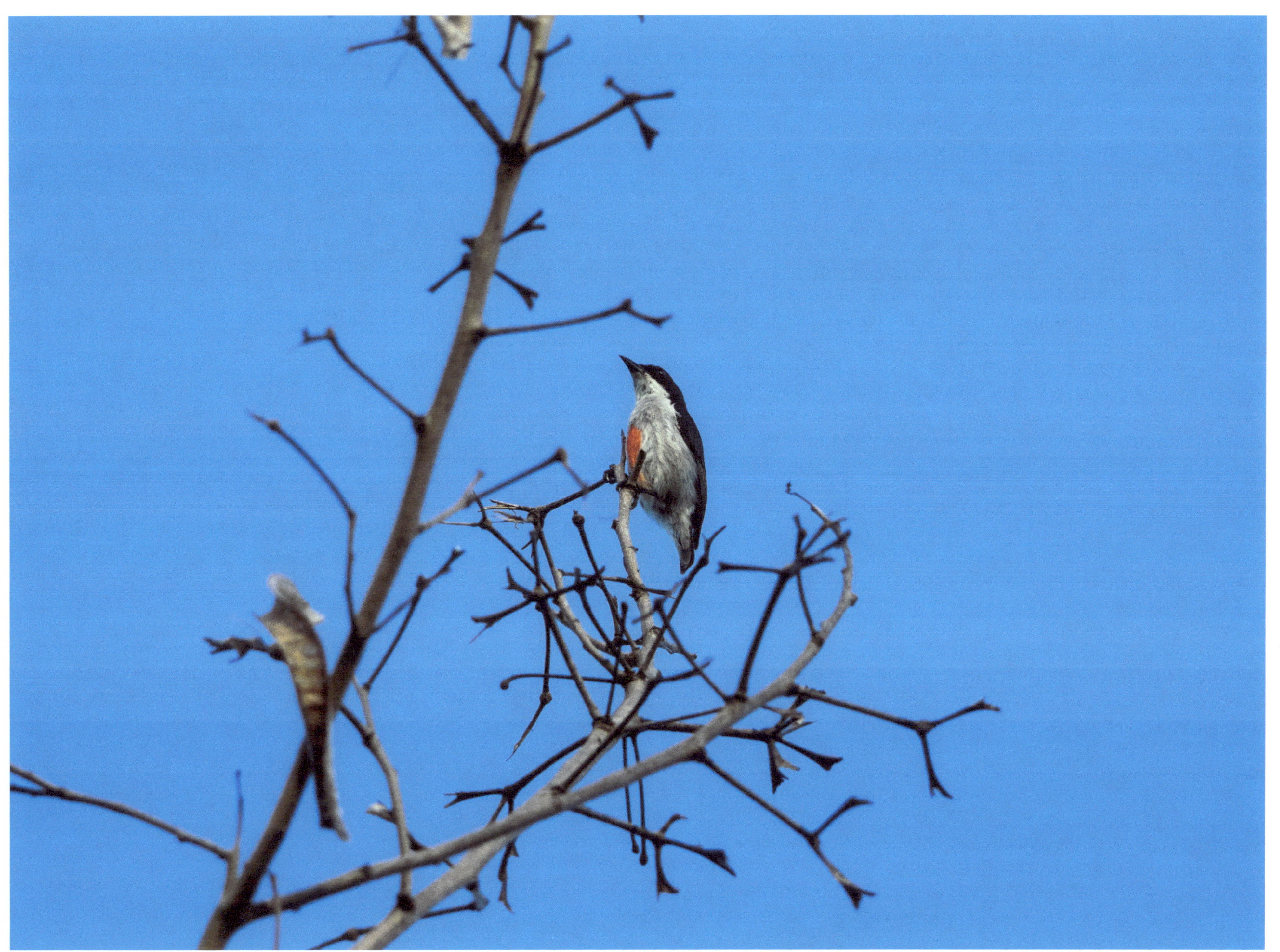

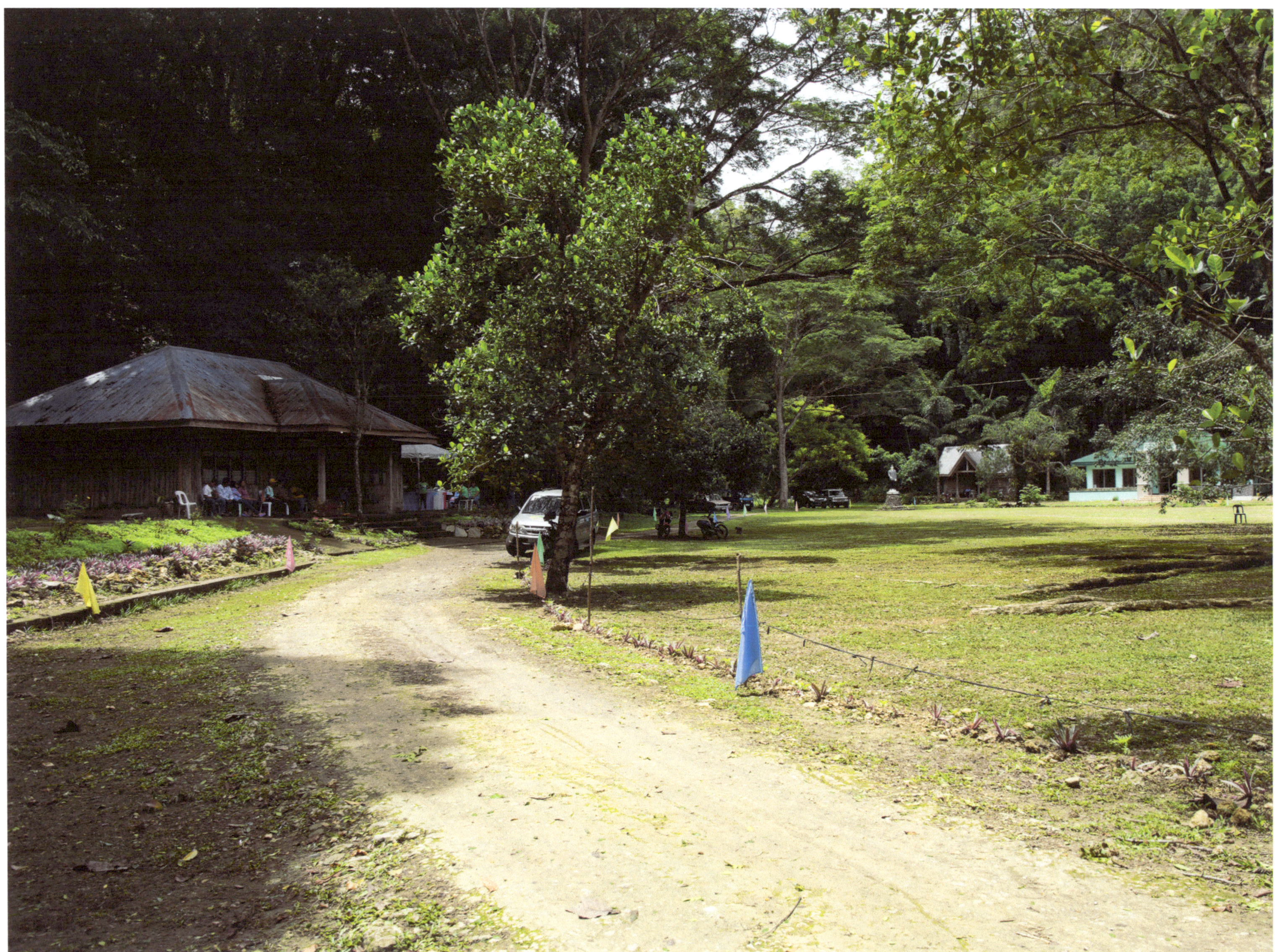

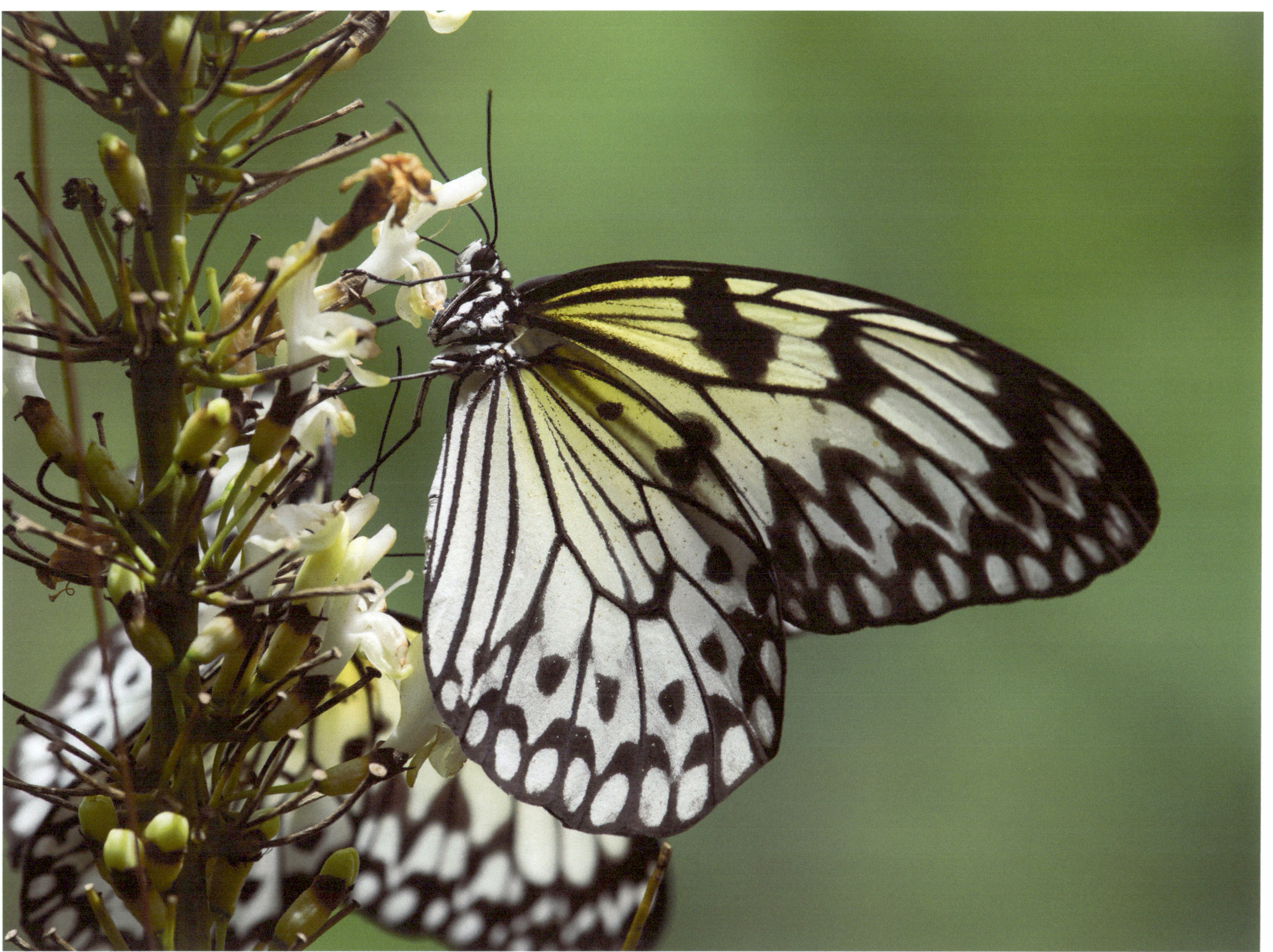

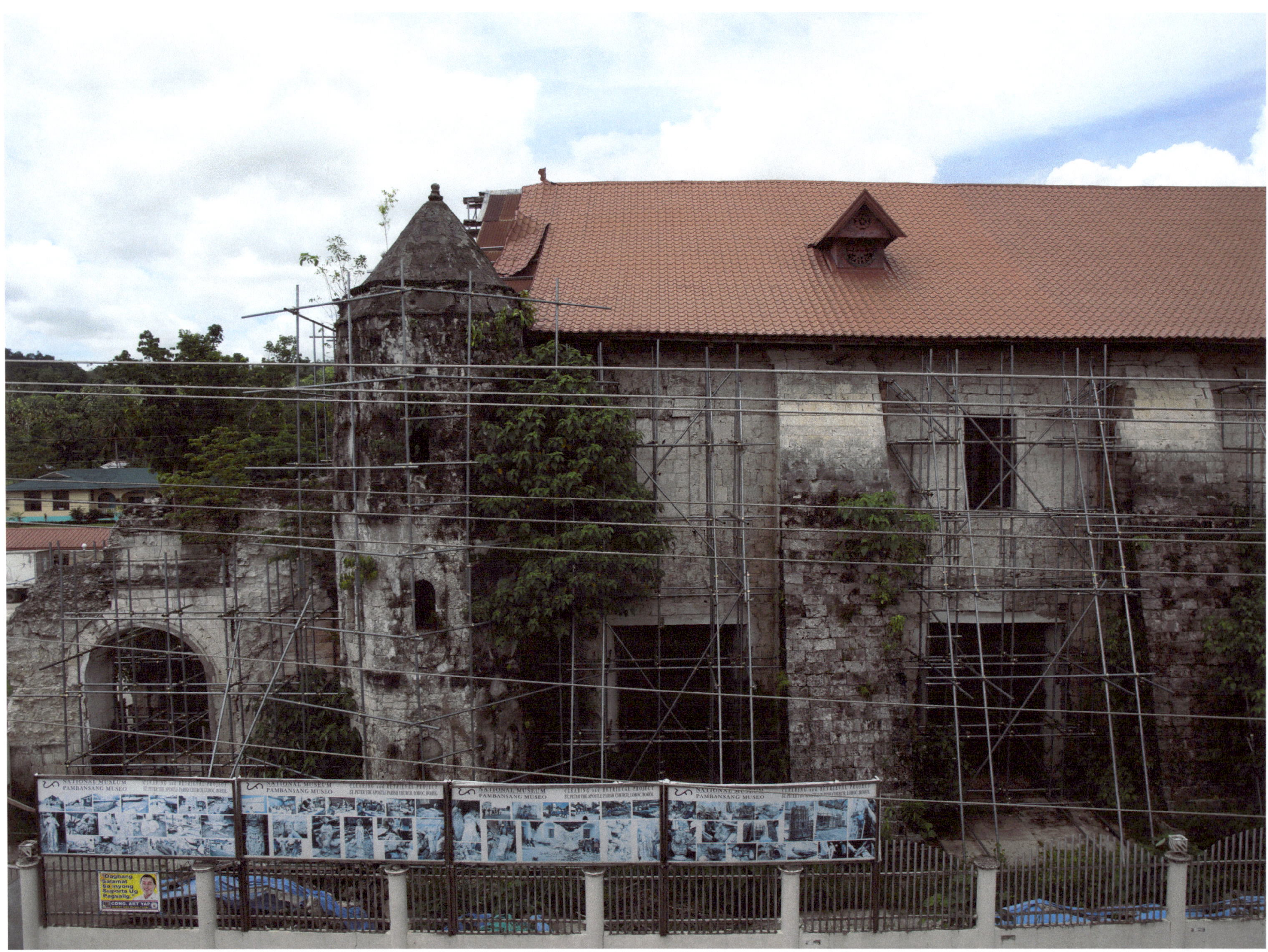
NATIONAL MUSEUM
PAMBANSANG MUSEO
"Daghang Salamat Sa Inyong Suporta Ug Pagsalig."
CONG. ART YAP

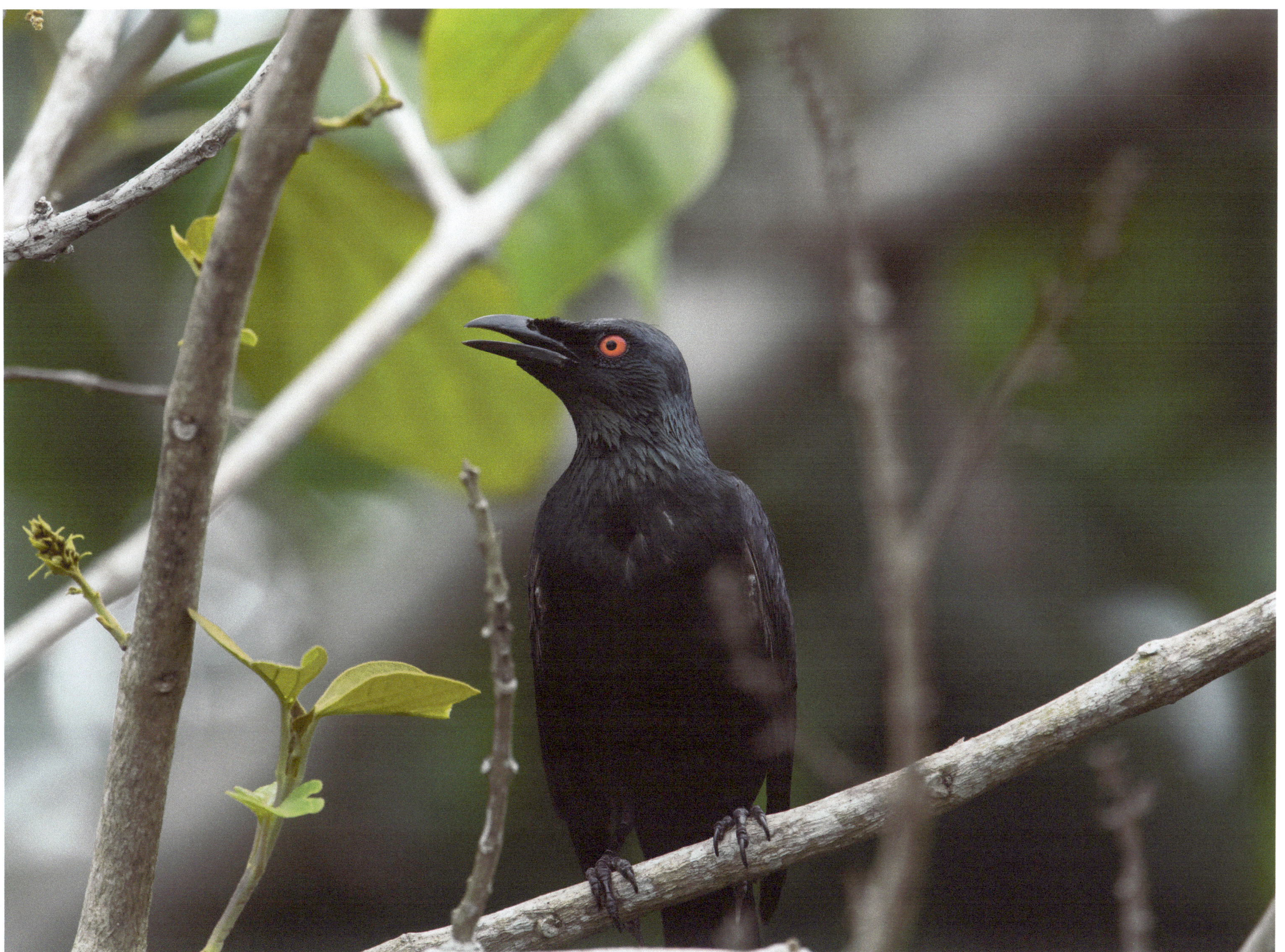

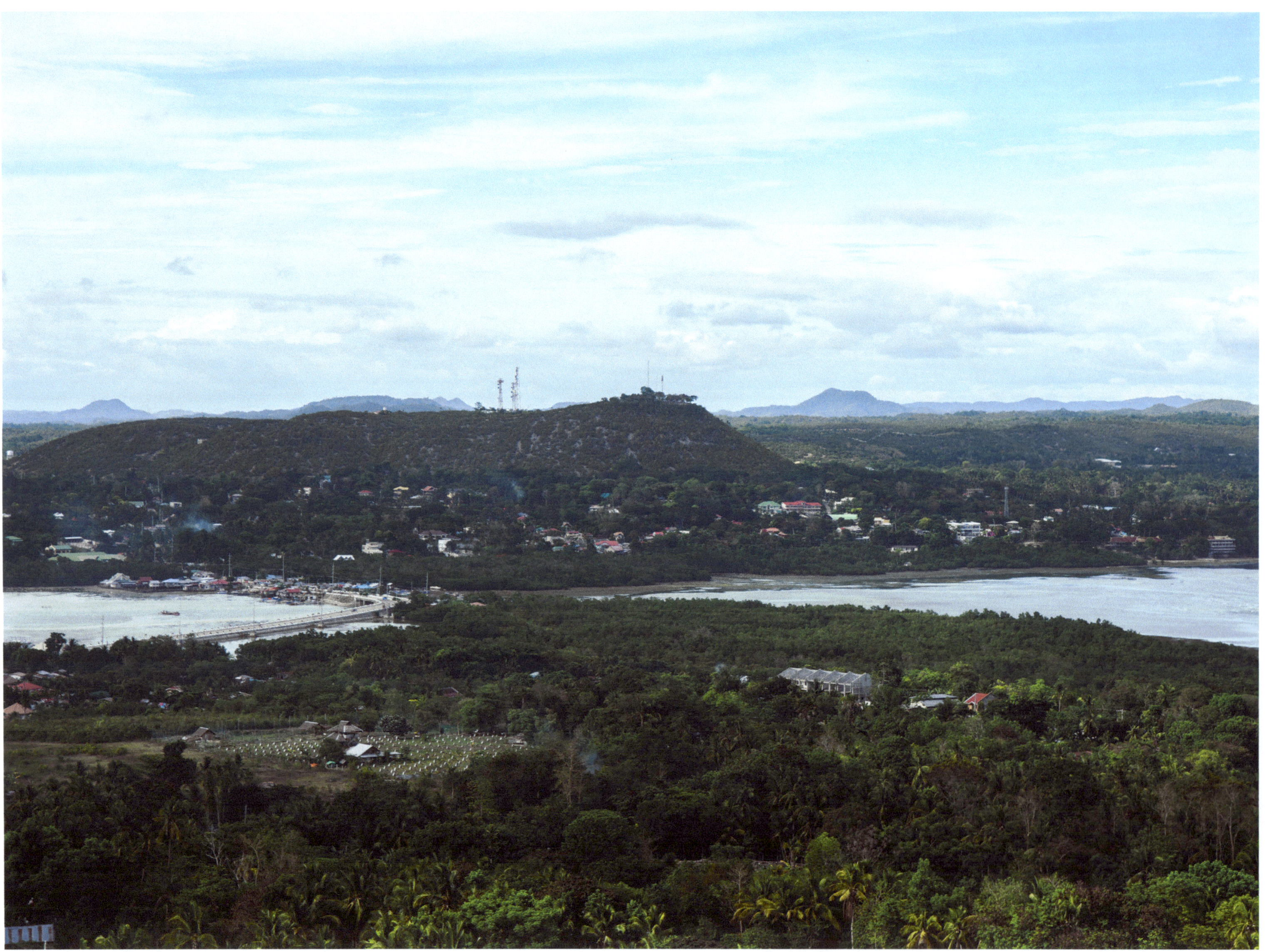

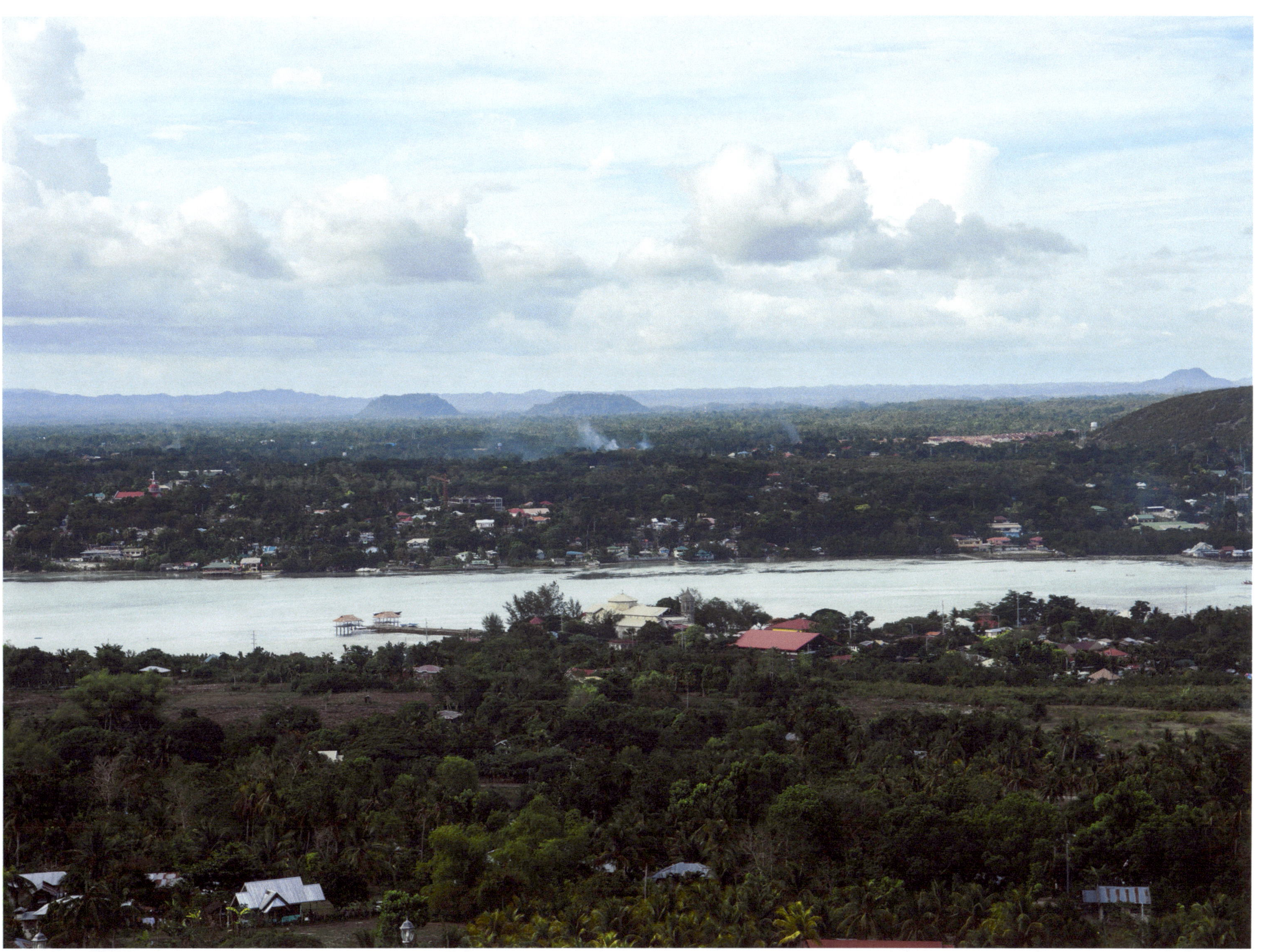

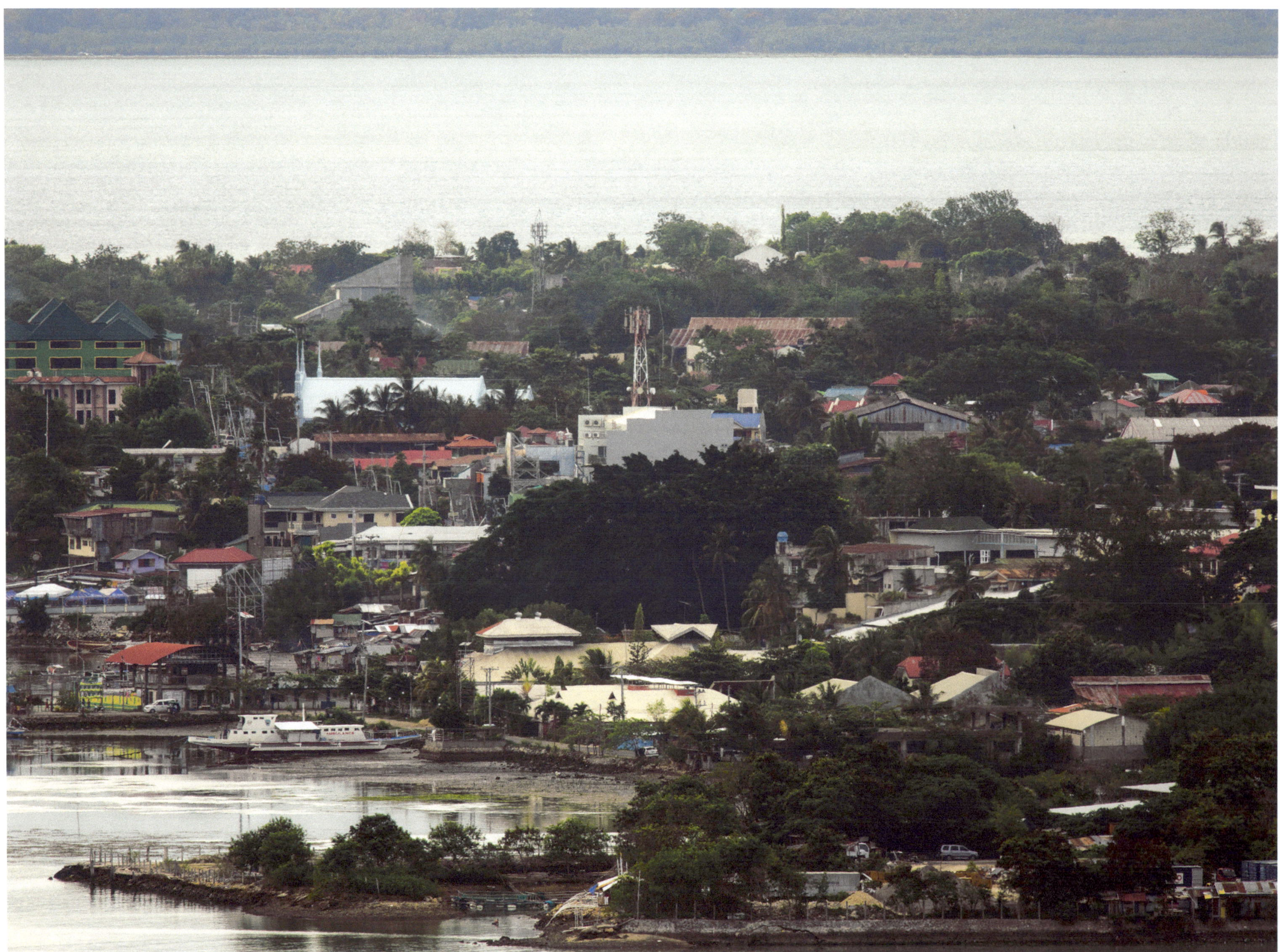

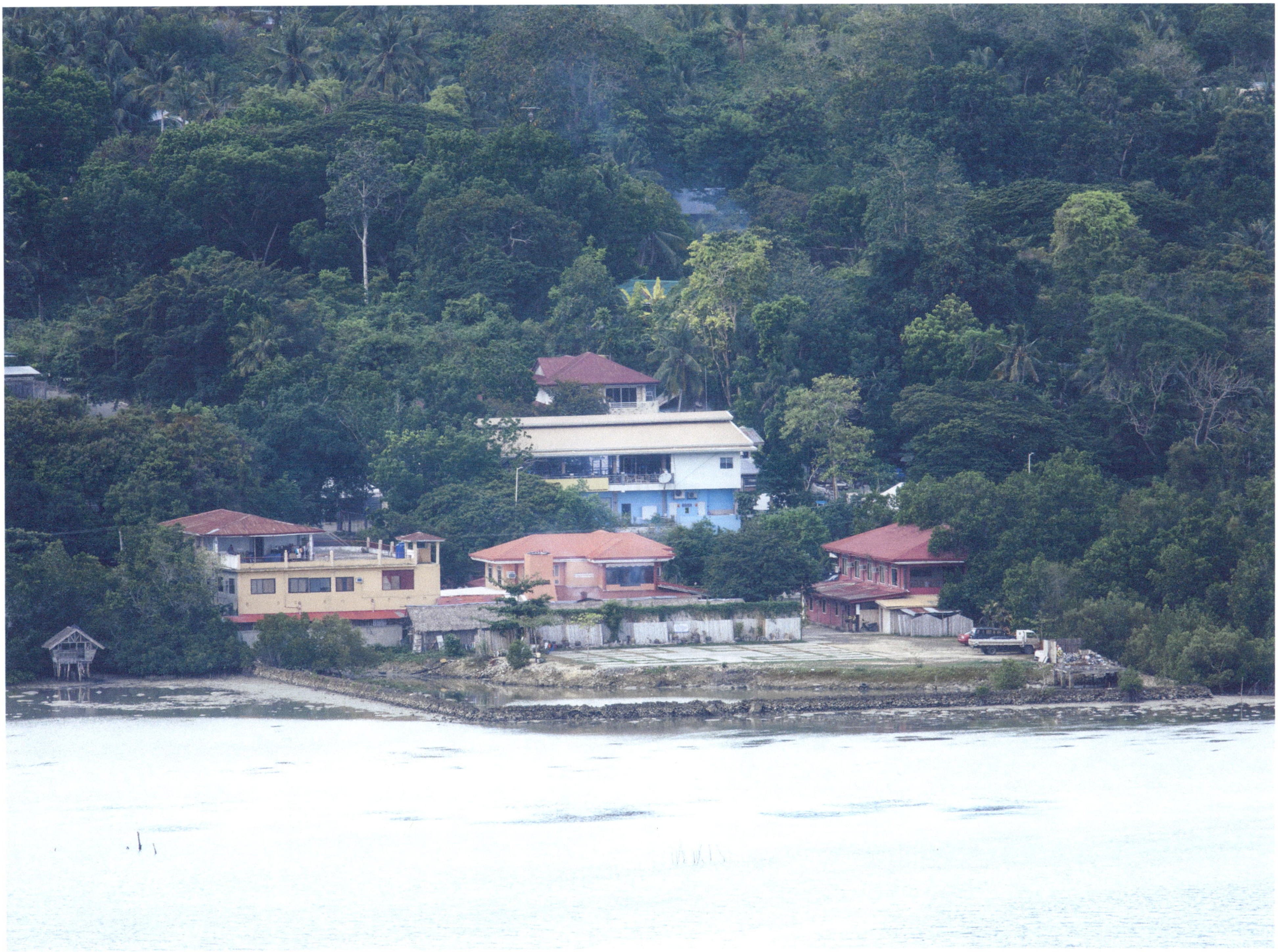

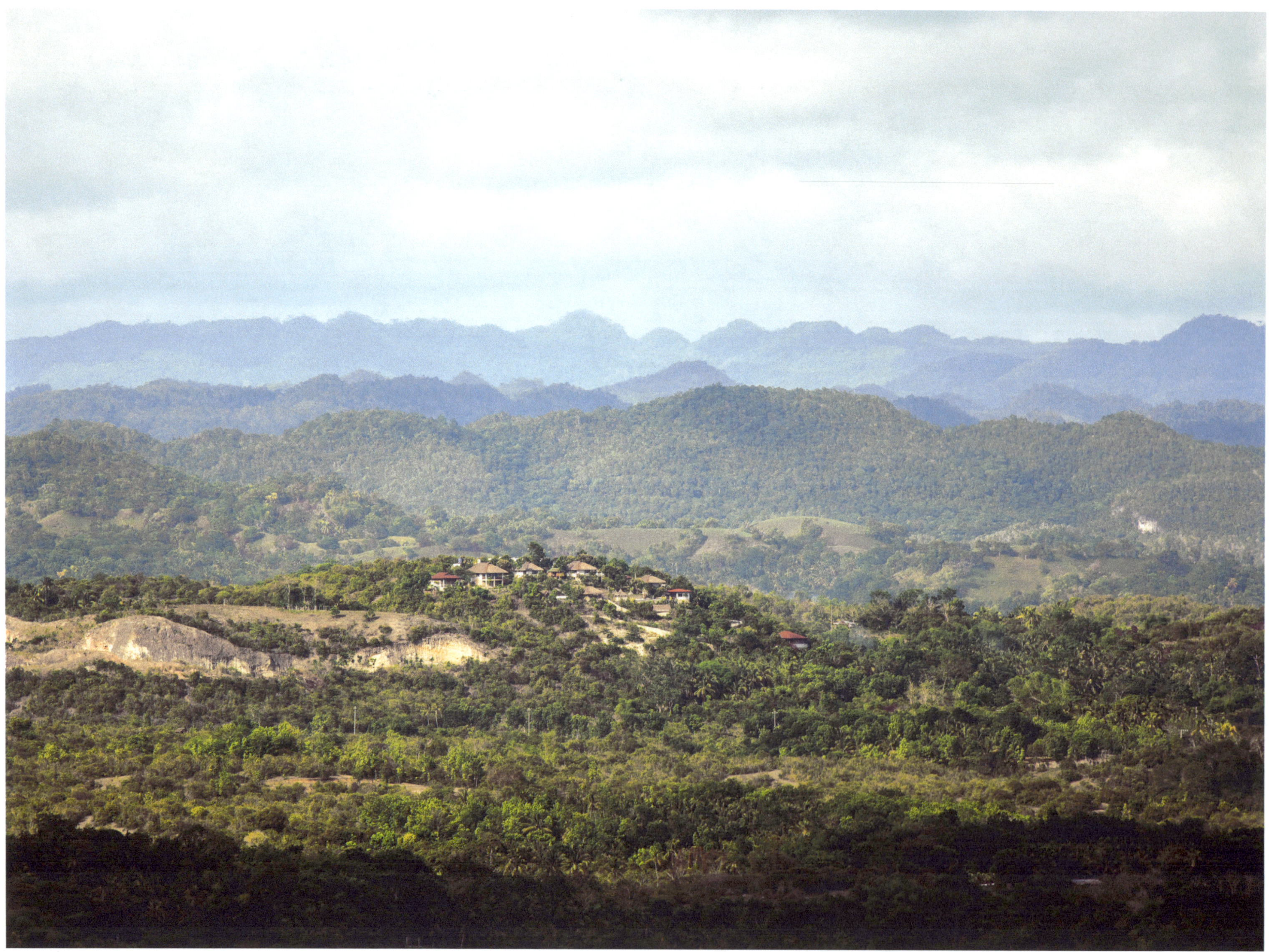

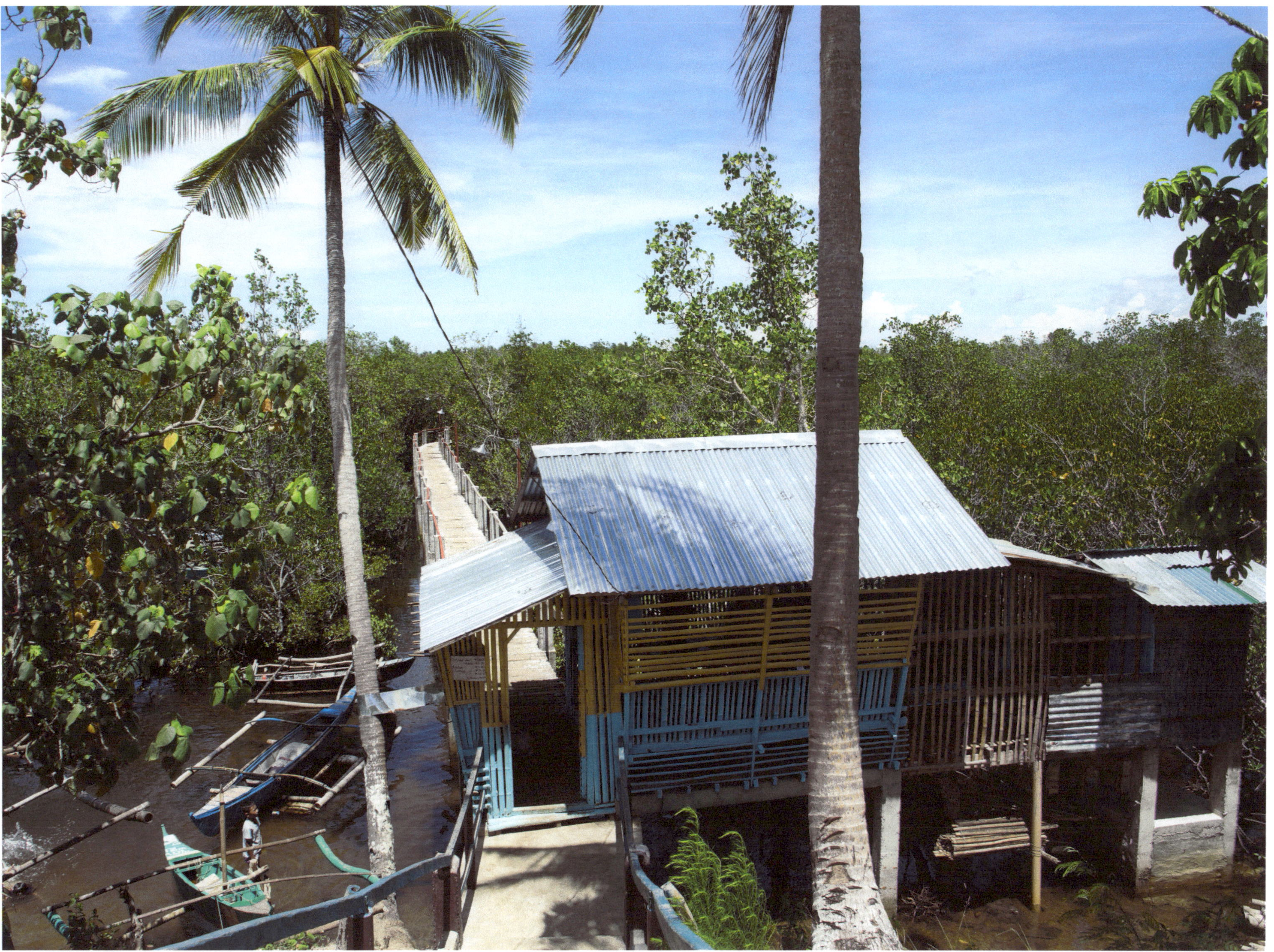

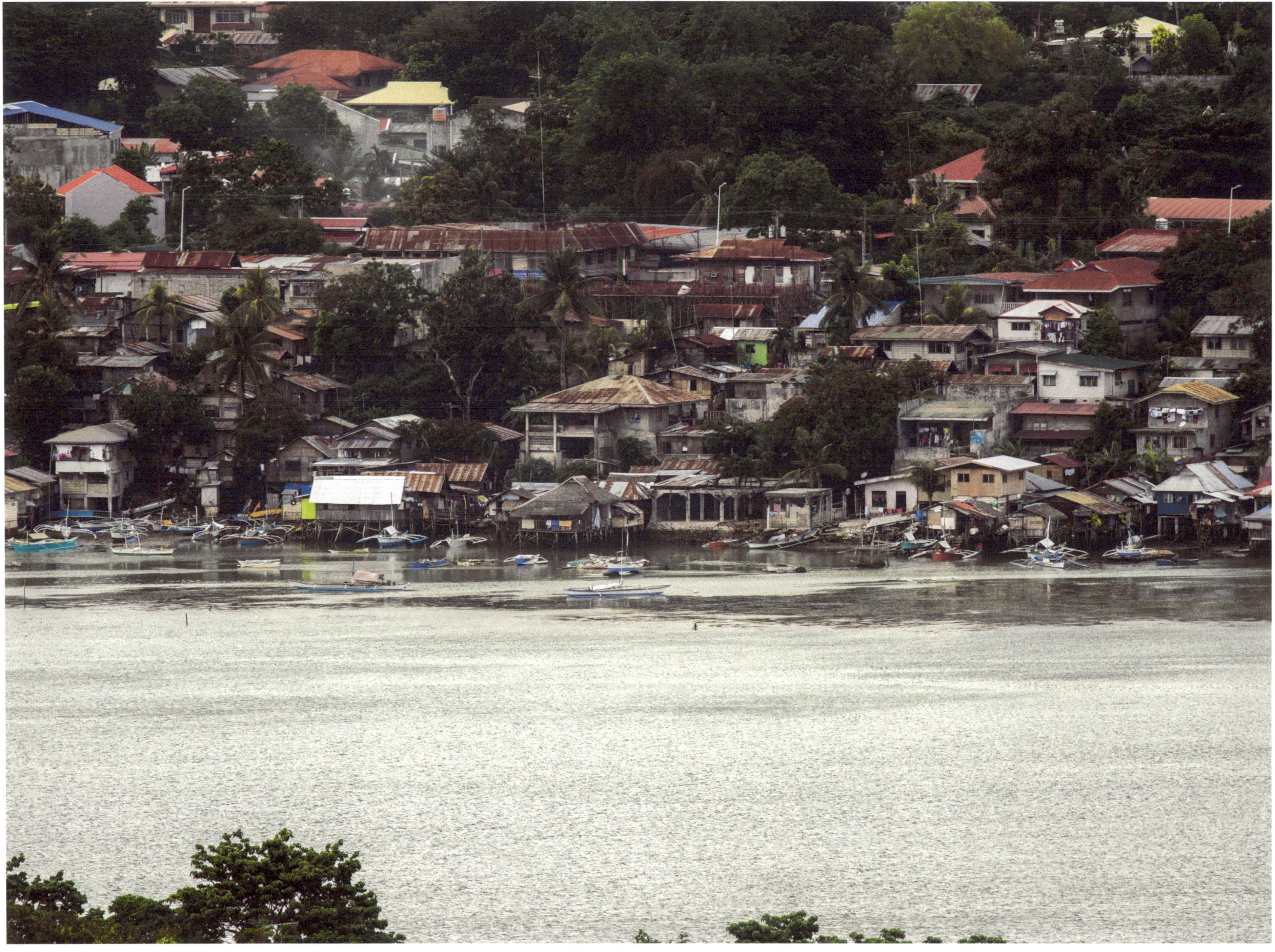

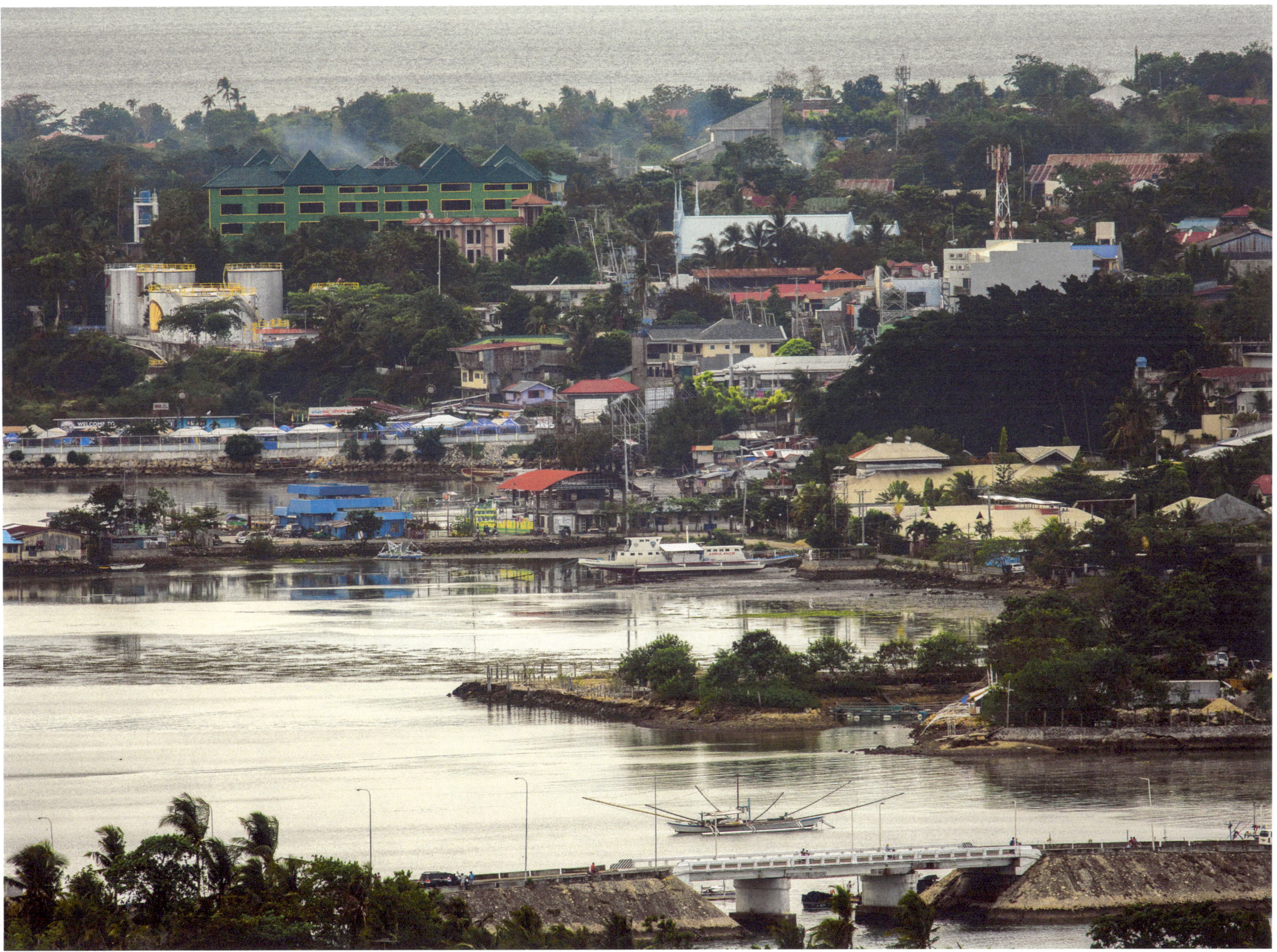
WELCOME TO
AMBULANCE

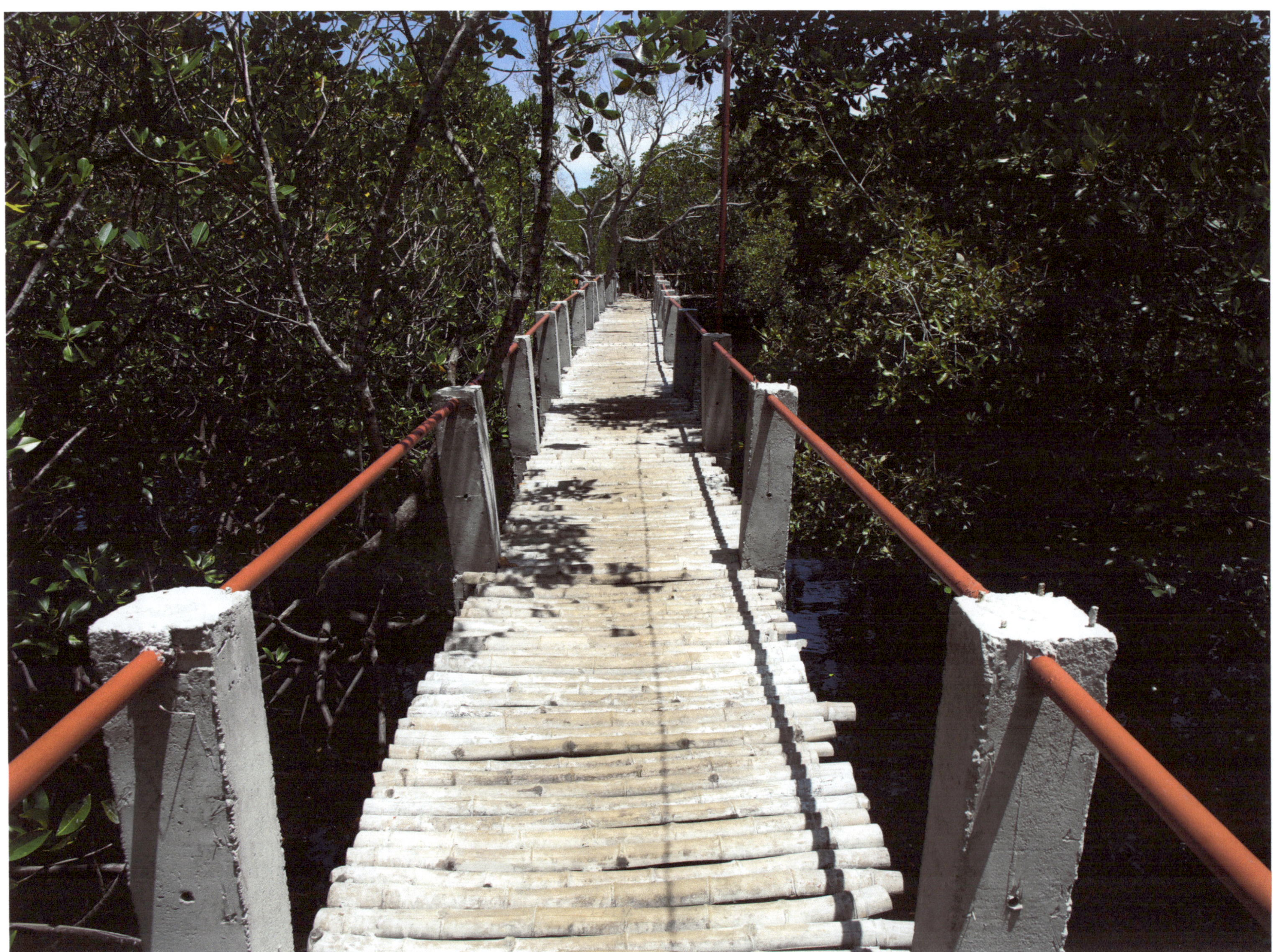

www.ingramcontent.com/pod-product-compliance
Lightning Source LLC
LaVergne TN
LVHW072330100826
845154LV00009B/148